ACTIVATE

THEA SPITZ

WESTBOW
PRESS®
A DIVISION OF THOMAS NELSON
& ZONDERVAN

WestBow Press books may be ordered through booksellers or by contacting:

WestBow Press
A Division of Thomas Nelson & Zondervan
1663 Liberty Drive
Bloomington, IN 47403
www.westbowpress.com
1 (866) 928-1240

ISBN: 978-1-5127-0329-0 (sc)
ISBN: 978-1-5127-0331-3 (hc)
ISBN: 978-1-5127-0330-6 (e)

Library of Congress Control Number: 2015911467

Print information available on the last page.

WestBow Press rev. date: 07/28/2015

CONTENTS

FOREWORD

I am so grateful to have the opportunity to introduce to you the book *Activate* by Thea Spitz. In churches, one of the common challenges is to get people engaged in sharing Christ and feeling equipped to fulfill Jesus's words to go into the entire world with the message of life.

I believe we are going into the world every day, but I don't believe we are making the impact that each believer has the potential to make.

Activate has a unique balance between personal stories and scriptural foundation keys for understanding areas of the Bible surrounding the salvation message. Clarifying what is God's part and what is our part in reaching the lost relieves some of the fear. Anyone who desires to lead people into a relationship with Jesus Christ can use several tools.

What I like best is that *Activate* gives leaders, teachers, and individuals entire outlines from which to teach and learn. This book is a great tool for local churches, small groups, and the person who wants to have a greater confidence to make a difference for the kingdom of God.

Bishop Randy Wooden
Kingdom Life Ministries
Lead Pastor

FOREWORD

It gives me great pleasure to introduce you to my friend Thea Spitz. When we first met, her name was Cynthia. When asked why she changed her name, she replied, "Well, Jesus took the sin out of my life, and I took the 'Cyn' out of my name."

Throughout the thirty-five years of our friendship, we continue to be so very grateful to our Father-God, who, in His unsearchable wisdom, placed us in the same Bible study group. It was a group of babes and toddlers in Christ who loved God, loved His Word, and loved each other. We had some awesome experiences as, led by the Holy Spirit, we went from being only a Bible study group to being a vibrant prayer group, where the Lord used Thea in the gifts of knowledge and wisdom and where every prayer was answered. Then the Lord connected us with two street evangelists, one whose station was the elite Rockefeller Center area, where we were challenged by the well-dressed professionals; and the other stationed at the corner of the Times Square and Forty-Second Street, where we learned to fearlessly share the gospel with people from all walks of life. It was indeed a glorious time.

As our spiritual lives developed and we each discovered our calling, we separated from each other to fulfill our purposes, and we hope to see all of the group in heaven and hear of the wonderful things that God has done through them.

But it was different with Thea and me. A lifelong friendship developed between us. Much to our surprise, we discovered in each other a kindred spirit—a most remarkable discovery, considering that Thea was a well-educated, middle-class, American-born white lady, and I was a black West Indian immigrant from a very poor background. We were both strong, independent, damaged women who had come to believe that being emotional was a weakness we couldn't afford to embrace. We used to laughingly declare that our mothers must have read the same parenting script. Our Christian journey also took us along similar paths. If it happened to Thea, then it was just a matter of time until it happened to me. It was wonderful having someone who understood me and could help me as I sought to "take off the old man and put on the new."

For Thea and me, physical separation was simply an inconvenience. We were separated by distance after eight years of knowing, loving, and depending on each other. Thea and her husband moved to Virginia, and I remained in New York, but we visited. Sixteen years later, I relocated to Trinidad, putting a whole ocean between us. Our love and friendship spanned the distances, and we often thank God for the technologies whereby we can keep in constant communication, sharing information and confidences, praying to and seeking God together, and always delighting in our similarities.

Thea Spitz is my friend, a person with whom I was/am able to share my ugliest secrets, deepest joys, sorrows, and hopes. She is my prayer partner and counselor whom I respect for her honesty in reproving and correcting me when it is necessary. God speaks to her and through her, and she may not want to expose what is wrong, reprimand, and charge because she does not like causing pain, but when God tells her, she tells me. "Faithful are the wounds of a friend; but the kisses of an enemy are deceitful" (Proverbs 27:6).

We know who we used to be and where we were headed, and we realize the amazing grace of God that changed us from lost to saved, from sinner to saint, from unholy to sanctified, and from ungodly to righteous. Our desire to be used by God to bring others out of darkness into the glorious light of the kingdom of God's Son grew strong in those early years. It was a time when people repented and accepted Jesus as both Savior and Lord, in the awareness of having grievously offended God, being powerless to cease from sin, and desperately desiring to live righteous, God-pleasing lives.

It was obvious in our early infancy and toddler days in Christ, when we "desired the sincere milk of the Word that we may grow thereby," that Thea's relationship with our Lord was deepening daily. She was definitely ahead of the rest of us in seeking God's face. As a young single woman, her full focus was God's Word and His will. She quickly went from a diet of milk to vegetables and meat, feeding on the undiluted Word of God with an insatiable hunger. God rewarded her diligent study with revelation knowledge and anointed her to be an evangelist, a teacher, and a prophet. Thea surrendered her all to Jesus Christ and, knowing that the Holy Spirit was leading her, she functioned with humility in those three offices. It was not God's will to exalt her into prominence, and so only eternity will reveal the many who sat under her ministry and were fully equipped to move on and serve God with confidence and excellence.

The preaching and teaching of the whole counsel of God, as revealed in the Holy Bible, without embellishment or subtraction, have always been of great concern to Thea. She cringes when the "itching ears" gospel is preached. She laments over the many souls who believe that they are saved and are on their way to heaven because they have repeated a prayer or have been baptized, even though they demonstrate no evidence of a changed life because there was no conviction of sin and therefore, there has been no repentance.

The awareness of the imminent trumpet call that will signal the home-going of the truly saved and the prompting of the Holy Spirit has driven Thea to write *Activate*.

Activate is a simple evangelistic tool that clearly leaves the Christian reader without an excuse for not being a part of the Great Commission. Indeed, it is an excellent study for Christians of any age and at any stage who desire to be obedient to the evangelistic call and feel ill equipped or lack the confidence to reach out to the unsaved and hell-bent people in their spheres of influence—family, friends, neighbors, educated, illiterate, young, or old.

Activate answers all objections and uncomplicates the process of sharing one's faith. It considers every philosophy of man and leads the reader to wisely and caringly declare the love and grace of God in response to man's sin and need.

Activate is the passionate response of a heart that expresses God's heart. "The Lord is not slack concerning his promise, as some men count slackness; but is longsuffering to us-ward, not willing that any should perish, but that all should come to repentance" (2 Peter 3:9).

Well done, Thea. May much fruit abound to you through the ministry of those who follow the teachings of *Activate*.

Dr. Andrea Palmer-Chase
Christian Counselor

INTRODUCTION:
THE UNWILLING AND THE UNPREPARED

If I were to mention the name of the prophet Jonah, most would think of the man who unwillingly spent several days of his life camped out in the belly of a fish. Jonah probably would have preferred to live a quiet life, maintaining a respectable image, participating in synagogue activities, and just being a godly example to the people of Galilee. Surely this would have been sufficient for a minister; God, however, had other plans.

The task God assigned to Jonah was to preach to the inhabitants of the Assyrian capital of Nineveh, located near the modern-day city of Mosul in Iraq. Assyria was a military threat to Israel, and reports of atrocities toward former conquests confirmed the Assyrians were both violent and cruel—they ruthlessly looted, maimed, enslaved, and killed on a mass scale. God called Jonah to leave his comfortable surroundings and warn the people of Nineveh to repent and believe in the God of Abraham, or they would soon face judgment. Jonah hated the assignment. Why should he care about the people in Nineveh? They were not his people but Gentiles—and nasty ones at that. All Assyrians were enemies of Israel and seeing them destroyed would be a major benefit, in his opinion. Jonah made up his mind; he was not going to Nineveh. Instead, he boarded a ship and began a journey in the opposite direction. If God wanted the people of Nineveh to be saved from destruction, He would have to choose someone else to accomplish the task. Jonah would not betray his country and help deliver a formidable enemy from a well-deserved divine judgment. When it came to the residents of Nineveh, Jonah's heart was cold, dead, and hardened. Jonah was the unwilling prophet.

Bob came into the office early that morning. He was eager to get to work and read the documentary material about company history, vision for the future, and of course, all about the boss and his accomplishments. Although he had been diligently studying the same book for a few years, it seems he was never able to master all there was to know about the chief executive officer (CEO) or the chief operations officer (COO) or even the chief of staff. They were distinguishable from one another but always worked in perfect unison to accomplish a task. For Bob, learning something new about them was nothing short of thrilling. It wasn't long after Bob's arrival that the COO entered the room and spoke to him. "Got a minute?" he asked. Bob's heart beat a little faster at this opportunity to enter the boss's office and speak face-to-face. Of course, the COO had talked with Bob before and each time had proved a positive and enlightening experience. Bob loved the boss with all his heart, and there was nothing he could ask that Bob would not be willing to do.

"I know you have been studying company documentation diligently, but why haven't you done what I asked you to do?" The boss didn't project anger, just disappointment. Bob felt a deep sadness flood his entire being. The thought of failing to do a job for the one he dearly loved really hurt. He knew exactly what the boss was referring to; he could offer no excuse except the stumbling block created by his own feelings of inadequacy and unpreparedness. In fact, that is why he was so diligent about studying the company documents. He wanted to become skilled in sharing information, both about the company and the boss. But the boss was 100 percent correct: studying and doing were two different things. In his heart, Bob saw himself as an effective evangelist, eloquently sharing the gospel of Jesus Christ with everyone who would listen. However, the essential fact is he failed to recognize opportunities until it was too late and the poignant moment had passed. He never actually walked through the open door, seizing the opportunity to tell others about the wonderful changes in his life because of the boss. If the whole truth were told, he was afraid to open his mouth.

The Purpose of *Activate*

Activate is a training manual suitable for anyone willing to follow the Lord's command. *Activate* is not for the hard-hearted Jonahs who do not care about the spiritual welfare of others. The Lord will deal with these folks individually, hopefully with less drastic methods than a three-day trip in the belly of a great fish. *Activate* is written for the Bobs, who want to be obedient to the Lord but lack experience. *Activate* will help identify the mission field, help develop a plan, and confront possibly intimidating stumbling blocks. Following the narrative of each chapter is a detailed outline, designed for class discussion and teaching small groups. *Activate* is an excellent motivational resource for Christians at any stage of their spiritual journeys. While we are not all called to a foreign mission field, we are called to point to Jesus as the only way of salvation. Your mission, should you choose to accept it, is outreach, and your mission field is on your own doorstep.

CHAPTER ONE

Digging Out from under "Me"

On November 22, 2014, residents of Buffalo, New York, woke to find they were inundated with snow. The actual accumulation measured eighty-eight inches (that's more than seven feet), setting a new record for the area. Later that morning, photos were posted on the Internet, showing just what seven feet of snow looked like. Door frames and windows were shattered under the weight, and only the most solid construction survived the pressure. If your door was solid and opened outward, you were really stuck, but if you were fortunate enough to have a door that opened inward, the chances of digging out seemed better—that is, until you actually opened that door. When the door was opened, another door of solid snow remained. The imprint of the door's hardware and panels could be seen in the snow bank, and access, light, and fresh air were blocked. Obviously, nothing was getting in or out until the snow was removed.

The snowstorm triggered two lingering thoughts: first, that I am grateful to live in a warm climate; and second, that the snow exemplifies the effect of too much self in the life of a Christian. Self-focus is a mockery, appearing to offer a genuine door but instead functioning as a blockade, preventing spiritual light and fresh air from entering. The air inside can quickly become stale and the light prove insufficient without the flow of the Word and the Spirit. Any attempt to reach out with the gospel is severely crippled until the snowstorm of self is removed.

Snow Job—Set Up for Failure

We've been set up for failure. Even within the company of true believers in Jesus Christ, the effects of self-centeredness have hindered spiritual growth and curtailed meaningful evangelism. Fostering selfishness has proven to be good business. Mega-churches continue to grow by focusing on how following Jesus will make you feel great and cause you to flourish. They're not telling lies, exactly, just emphasizing the benefits and ignoring the costs of discipleship. The apostle Paul warned Timothy that these things would happen, and we are seeing a clear demonstration of his words coming to pass in our time. Paul used the expression, "itching ears" to illustrate the focus on making the hearer feel good and comfortable without regard for truth.

> For the time will come when they will not endure
> sound doctrine; but after their own lusts shall they heap
> to themselves teachers, having itching ears; (2 Tim. 4:3)

An entire generation has been carefully conditioned to strive to fulfill private lusts. For the benefit of Christians, a smokescreen of spirituality mitigates the raw selfishness with promises of how personal success enables the financing of ministry endeavors. A major US company used the concept of scratching those "itching ears" in advertising campaigns. Their slogan correctly identified the target audience as the Me generation. Although, technically the Me generation is defined as Americans born during the 1946 to 1964 baby boom, the attitude of excessive selfishness extends to those born well beyond the confines of that definition. For our purposes, the Me generation will include all those born after 1946.) While the emphasis on self has been magnified in our culture, there have always been those who followed Jesus for the goodies. Many of today's "Bless me, Lord" recruits bear a close resemblance to the crowd who flocked to Jesus for miracles and free bread. Jesus exposed their motives and clearly outlined the truly devastating requirement for following Him. This is so important it is recorded in three gospels: Matthew 16:24, Mark 8:34, and Luke 9:23.

> Then said Jesus unto his disciples, If any man will come after me, let him deny himself, and take up his cross, and follow me. (Matt. 16:24)

The problem is that the truth about denying self is just not good business. When the going gets tough, those who signed on for prosperity and good feelings will find it hard to endure. If, in the days when Jesus was bodily present, casual followers left Him when His words offended them, how much more will they leave the congregations of today? Only Jesus's true disciples continued with Him, pledging their allegiance to the Son of the living God (John 6:68–69).

It is not a pleasing thought, but for all followers of Jesus, trouble and persecution are givens. The apostle Paul advised his spiritual son Timothy that "all those who live godly in Christ Jesus shall suffer persecution" (2 Tim. 3:12). Jesus addressed the consequences of not being prepared. In a parable recorded in Mark 4, He talked of the rapid departure of those who became offended by tribulation and persecution because they had no root in the Word of God. When we do not teach the cost of discipleship because it may offend, we are not really making disciples. Those who are not prepared to take up their crosses will fall away from the faith when trouble comes their way.

The Worldview of the Me Generation

Before we even think about reaching out to others, we need to settle our personal relationship with the Lord. Like the snow in Buffalo, we need to get self out of the way, so we have enough light to see where we are going and so the glory of the Lord can shine through us. This may be even more difficult for the Me generation than for people of the past, because self-focus has become so much a part of our worldview. It is a record snowstorm, indeed.

The apostle Paul talked at length about a war that goes on inside all of us. The flesh is at war with the spirit. Our flesh seeks personal gain, the spotlight, and doing all things our way. Selfishness is a major stumbling block, preventing a true and compelling commitment to Jesus Christ because we are really committed to ourselves. The dictionary definition of selfishness is, "concerned excessively or exclusively with oneself: seeking or concentrating on one's own advantage, pleasure, or well-being without regard for others." [1] Psychologists classify the root of selfishness as a lack of empathy; an inability to see the viewpoint of another.

Born That Way

It is true that babies are born selfish. As we grow, however, we should learn that we are not the center of the universe. Past generations taught biblical values of preferring others at a very early age (Phil. 2:3; Rom. 12:10). This doctrine was reinforced in school, where other children were brought into the child's world, and the concept of teamwork became real. Calling an inordinate amount of attention to oneself was discouraged, and positive attention had to be earned through achievement. Students had rights, of course, but along with those rights came responsibilities to others.

Somehow our society has migrated away from teaching responsibility. Schools seem to encourage selfishness, teaching our children about their entitlements from a tender age. Special awards are given for doing what is simply the right thing and not breaking the rules. When my niece was in school, she was awarded student-of-the-month status simply for showing up for class. Although I didn't intend to hurt her feelings, I was shocked at the low criterion for the award. She was crushed when I asked her, "Isn't that what you are supposed to do?" My concern is that after graduation, there are no awards given for just showing up. It is difficult for the child of entitlement to grasp that life is competitive, and rewards must be earned. A greater problem is created when the

---

[1]   Selfish [Def. 1]. (n.d.). In *Merriam Webster Online,* Retrieved June 20,2015, from http://www.merriam-webster.com/dictionary/selfish.

entitlement generation is not given all it believes is its right to receive. The result is frustration and anger. Selfishness cries out, "Get what is owed you."

The spirit of entitlement has overflowed into the church. "Coming to Jesus" for the children of entitlement means collecting what they believe is owed them; namely, prosperity, health, a free pass to get out of hell, and everything else included in the "abundant life" package. What? Take up the cross to follow Him? Not likely!

Good Business Capitalizes on Bad Self-Image

Focus on self-image is all around us. It is good business. Endless beauty and fitness infomercials keep us immersed in our shortcomings, which we are willing to spend dollars to overcome. Self-help is a profitable sub-segment of best-selling nonfiction books. There are also numerous self-help websites to aid in fixing whatever you believe is wrong with you—for a price. The by-product of intense self-focus is the opposite of the intent; it's a manifestation of a poor self-image. In part, feelings of inadequacy come from an attempt to achieve an impossible and stereotypical physical image. Gyms, diets, and pharmaceutical miracles reap financial benefits as people strive to achieve Barbie-doll shapes and six-pack abs. The collapse occurs because personal value comes from our success or failure in conforming to an impossible physical image. We are only as good as we look, and since aging inevitably affects appearance, we are unavoidably set up for a poor self-image, no matter how hard we work. The standard definition of self-esteem is a feeling of worth based on skills, accomplishments, status, financial resources, or appearance. The worldly view of self-esteem is quite unscriptural but has crept into the church, damaging many.

Society's Remedy Applied by the Church

Our culture blames many social problems on poor self-image and low self-esteem. Their solution is that if people improve their self-images, they will feel better about themselves and perform better in life. This bogus and nonbiblical line of thought has deceived church leaders into making the building of self-esteem a goal of the church. The hope was it would enable those who love themselves to love God. That logic is deceptive, switching the priorities of the first and second commandments given by Jesus. First, we are to love the Lord our God with all our hearts, minds, souls, and strength, and after that, love our neighbor as ourselves (Matt. 6:33). The church needs to reestablish loving God as a priority, and improved self-image will follow.

Bursting the Self-Esteem Bubble

A study conducted at the Florida State Prison exposed something very interesting about self-esteem and its effect on behavior in society. The study evaluated the self-esteem of convicted felons. The outcome poked a big hole in the concept of low self-esteem as the cause of societal woes. Professor Roy F. Baumeister, a psychology professor at Florida State University, found the most violent offenders were the most narcissistic and had the greatest perceived levels of self-esteem. High self-esteem people showed little self-control when things did not go their way. They appear to have no respect for others.

What Happens When Rights Collide

The "Me" generation has been carefully schooled to know and insist upon rights. If my rights are to have what I want when I want it, then it is inevitable that my rights will eventually collide with yours. What happens when personal rights contradict one another? Who survives the collision? We like to think that good will prevail, but unfortunately the survivor is usually the one with the most political clout. In 1973 the Supreme Court found a "right to privacy" hidden somewhere in the US Constitution. Based on this decision, a "right" to terminate the life of an unborn baby became the law of the land. The preborn baby was dehumanized and accorded no rights at all because, allegedly, a woman could do what she wanted with her own body. Even the most basic right to life is abrogated in favor of the more powerful social force. We have become so obsessed with "rights" that we lack empathy for the unborn. This fits the core definition of selfishness: excessive concern with oneself, and having little regard for others. Where are those who recognize responsibilities toward others?

Where Is the Church?

The kind of selfishness that permits a mother to legally kill her unborn child is not confined to secular society. Some churches actually close their eyes to the evil of abortion considering it a viable answer to unwanted pregnancies. A few years ago, I read a segment of a handbook produced at the annual meeting of a major denomination. It contained a ministerial standard supporting abortion that began, "If after prayerful consideration, a woman is led to terminate a pregnancy ..."

Other forms of behavior directly violating the scriptural standards are ignored in favor of filling the pews with warm bodies. Confronting sin in the church is avoided because we wouldn't want to make a "seeker" feel uncomfortable. This is an outgrowth of the dangerous focus on self that has crept into the church. Anything is acceptable as long as we are "seeker-friendly" and we make our parishioners comfortable.

What is the answer? The Word of God is a safeguard against selfishness only if we follow what it says. Paul had to take strong action in the Corinthian church when immorality threatened the integrity of the body of Christ. His decision was not based on an individual's comfort or even on his own reputation but on the standards set forth in God's Word (1 Cor. 5). When we take our eyes off ourselves and focus on Jesus and His requirement to deny ourselves and take up our cross to follow Him ... well, there go all our rights and entitlements.

Facing Our Own Selfishness First

Self-focus plays a major part in hindering personal outreach with the gospel of Jesus Christ. There will be times when you will be very uncomfortable and times you will experience rejection and even ridicule. That is why you must face your selfishness first. Your personal value system must be examined and your commitment to the Lord evaluated in the light of the cross. Peter proudly proclaimed that he was ready to follow Jesus, even to death, but when the "rubber hit the road," so did Peter. His self-examination came about when Jesus asked him, "Simon, do you love me more than these?" (John 21:15–19). Are you prepared to answer that same question?

Self-Examination

Psychologists often attribute the ills of our society to a lack of self-esteem, but it is more likely that poor self-esteem is a by-product of engaging in what the Bible calls the "works of the flesh." Flesh has quite a product list.

> Now the works of the flesh are manifest, which are
> these; Adultery, fornication, uncleanness, lasciviousness,
> Idolatry, witchcraft, hatred, variance, emulations,
> wrath, strife, seditions, heresies, envyings, murders,
> drunkenness, revellings, and such like: of the which I
> tell you before, as I have also told you in time past, that
> they which do such things shall not inherit the kingdom
> of God. (Gal. 5:19–21)

We cannot blame the problems in society on God, nor can we blame them on the Devil (although he loves to see them happen). The book of James clearly shows that we are responsible for the works of the flesh when we are drawn away of our desires.

> Let no man say when he is tempted, I am tempted of
> God: for God cannot be tempted with evil, neither
> tempteth he any man: But every man is tempted, when
> he is drawn away of his own lust, and enticed. Then
> when lust hath conceived, it bringeth forth sin: and
> sin, when it is finished, bringeth forth death. (James
> 1:13–15)

Look in the Mirror, Not at Anyone Else

It is easy to spot selfishness in other people but very difficult to recognize it in ourselves. Take a look in the mirror and check yourself out. The following compound words may shed light on your own areas of difficulty:

1- **Self-centeredness**: Does everything revolve around you? Do all of your goals revolve around self-promotion? Are you the center of the universe? How do your attitudes and goals line up with "Seek ye first the kingdom of God and His righteousness" (Matt. 6:33)? A key to recognizing self-centeredness in yourself is counting the number of times you say "me," "my," "I," or "mine" in your testimony.

2- **Self-Conceit:** when that "can-do" attitude is based upon your own abilities. Self-conceit is an inflated estimation of your own ability to complete the task. Earlier generations referred to self-conceit by a simpler name: pride. Pride is one of the things the Bible clearly states God hates. God hates pride and resists the proud (Prov. 16:18; James 4:6, 10; Luke 18:14). Paul warned against self-conceit in the book of Romans. He said we are not to think too highly of self (Rom. 12:3). Paul was a man of superior natural ability, yet he resolved to depend entirely on the Lord (1 Cor. 2:2).

3- **Self-Will:** Self-willed people are stubborn and must have their own way. There is danger for the self-willed of mistaking personal will for the will of God. This is something on which the Enemy loves to capitalize, because the stubborn person can be manipulated and deceived. Instead of submitting our will to God, we twist and contort the Word of God to fit our own desires. Even when a self- willed person is not deceived, he is in danger of losing out by asserting personal will. Remember the prophet Jonah? God told him to go to Nineveh and preach, but Jonah's will was to see Nineveh judged instead of saved, and so he fled. He had to become dinner for a fish in order to submit his will.

4- **Self-Indulgence:** doing your own thing in pursuit of pleasure and avoidance of pain. Self-indulgent people will not be able to stand firm when their faith is challenged. They are like the seed Jesus described in the parable of the sower (Matt. 13:13). The desire for personal comfort will hinder anything the self-indulgent attempts.

5– **Self-Righteousness**: evaluating yourself according to your own standards and deciding you are righteous. The most glaring biblical examples of self-righteousness are the Pharisees (Luke 18:9–14; Rom. 10:1–3). They did not see their own sin and considered themselves far above their countrymen for the scrupulous way they thought they kept the Law of Moses. They even accused Jesus of fraternizing with sinners (Matt. 9:10–12). It must have been a "mind-blower" for the Pharisees when Jesus announced His mission was not directed to them but to the very people they had so painstakingly ignored (Luke 5:32). We are all included in the set of transgressors for whom Jesus came. Before the righteousness of Christ can be imputed to us, we must stop evaluating our own righteousness and acknowledge personal sin (2 Cor. 5:21). In the eyes of many Christians, Paul was one of the greatest followers of the Lord, yet he was the complete antithesis of self-righteousness. He considered himself "chief of sinners" (1 Tim. 1:15).

6– **Self-Satisfaction:** This is a major obstacle facing the church in our generation. Another word for self-satisfaction is complacency; being content with the status quo. Self-satisfied Christians do not want to know what is going on around them and are just waiting for the Lord to rescue them from all that is unpleasant in this world. Complacent Christians accept mediocrity and excuse themselves from service. They do nothing to advance the kingdom of God. How can we reach out to the unsaved and make disciples, as the Lord commanded, if we bury ourselves in our own contentment? Paul serves as our godly example, the antithesis of self-satisfaction. He was always seeking to be better, striving to do more, that Jesus may be glorified.

"Brethren, I count not myself to have apprehended: but this one thing I do, forgetting those things which are behind, and reaching forth unto those things which are before, I press toward the mark for the prize of the high calling of God in Christ Jesus" (Phil. 3:13–14).

How to Dig Out from Under the Snow of Self

If any of the above areas of self focus apply to you, the next logical question is, how do you get free? Paul gives us the key. He advises that we consider ourselves as dead to sin and that includes the sin of selfishness (Rom. 8:11).

Putting "self" to death is accomplished by denying yourself, esteeming others better than yourself (Phil. 2:3; John 13:3–17), and humbling yourself before God (1 Peter 5:6). As Jesus became the sacrifice for our sin, we are invited to bring Him glory by becoming a living sacrifice unto God. Only then can we give ourselves to the good works prepared for us from the foundation of the world (2 Cor. 8:5; Rom. 12:1–2). How do we do these things? Words roll off the tongue easily, but accomplishment is difficult. In order to truly put selfishness to death, we must learn the skill of taking authority over our thought life and bringing every thought into conformity with the will of God. This is an ongoing battle, but victory is achievable (Prov. 16:32; Gal. 5:23; 2 Peter 1:6). Like any other skill, our success ratio increases the more we practice. In this battle, self-centeredness becomes God-centeredness, self-will submits to God's will, and self-satisfaction becomes the satisfaction of the victory we share in Christ Jesus.

God-living each day to accomplish the good works for which they were created so that Father and Son might be glorified in them.

Study/Teaching Outline: Digging Out from Under "Me"

1- Defining the Problem
   • Definition of selfishness: chiefly concerned with self and self-interests above the well-being of others
   • An inordinate focus on "me, myself, I, and my way"
   • Psychologists say the root of selfishness is a "lack of empathy."
2- How our society encourages selfishness.
   • Commercial focus of advertising—the Me generation

- Endless infomercials selling beauty and fitness
- Self-help material becomes subject matter for best-sellers.
- Examples of titles from the Internet, list of 100 best-selling books:
  - *From Panic to Power*: promises to help calm your anxieties
  - *How to Make People Like You in 90 Seconds*: convincing others you are likeable
  - *When I Say No, I Feel Guilty*: help in not accepting blame for problems of others
  - *Re-inventing Your Life*: help stop negative behavior
- Capitalizing on poor self-image
- Poor self-image is a big seller for diets.
- Improve self-image by striving to conform to an impossible norm.
  - Acquiring a "Barbie-doll" shape.
  - Acquiring "six-pack abs" like a superhero.
- Society blames social problems on poor self-image, but closer examination reveals the root is the sin of selfishness. "I want what I want when I want it!"
- Society has become obsessed with "rights" based on selfishness..
- Example: abortion, the alleged "right" to do what you want with your body
- There is no concern for the right or life of the child.
- Schools foster a "spirit of entitlement" by stressing "rights."
- Overemphasis on rights—attitude becomes everyone owes me!
- Removes responsibility from the individual. You are responsible for yourself.
- Everyone rewarded equally, regardless of performance. Destroys incentive to succeed and punishes excellence.
- Proper attitude toward self is a sign of maturity.
- Followers of Jesus were told:, "If any man will come after me, let him deny himself and take up his cross, and follow me" (Matt. 16:24).
- There goes any entitlement you thought you had.

3- Biblical Examples of Selfishness and Sel<u>fless</u>ness

Selfish Examples: Try to identify the improper attitude toward self, the selfish action, and the consequences of selfish action.

- Cain (Genesis 4) had no regard for God or for the righteousness of his brother, Abel. Cain wanted honor for himself. His jealousy led to anger at his brother's success, and so he murdered him.
  - ◦ Cain's response to God demonstrates the *ultimate* selfishness.
  - ◦ "Am I my brother's keeper?" This rude and arrogant statement dishonors God.
  - ◦ Proper response to Cain's question is, *Yes,* we are our brother's keeper.
  - ◦ Our responsibility concerning the interests of others: "Let nothing be done through strife or vainglory; but in lowliness of mind let each esteem other better than themselves. Look not everyman on his own things, but every man also on the things of others" (Phil. 2:3–4).
  - ◦ Consequences of Cain's selfishness: murder of his brother; his own banishment (Gen 4:11–12).
- Ahab (1 Kings 21): Ahab, king of Israel, wanted to plant a garden in the land adjacent to his own. The problem was, the property was owned by Naboth, who refused to sell or to trade the vineyard because it was part of his ancestral inheritance.
  - ◦ Ahab sulked so much that his wife, Jezebel, took extraordinary steps to acquire the vineyard.
  - ◦ She "set up" Naboth, hiring false witnesses against him so that he would be stoned to death for blasphemy (1 Kings 21:11–14).
  - ◦ Naboth's property was seized, and Ahab got to plant vegetables.
  - ◦ Ahab asked no questions and showed no concern for how the vineyard was acquired or for Naboth or his family.

- ◦ Consequences of Ahab's selfishness: the murder of Naboth and the judgment of God against himself and all of his posterity (1 Kings 21:19–25).
- David, the king of Israel, had a close relationship with the Lord. The Lord blessed him with victories, wealth, and wives, as well as concubines. In spite of all this, David lusted after another man's wife (2 Sam. 11–-12).
  - ◦ David selfishly took what he wanted, knowing that Bathsheba was the wife of Uriah the Hittite (2 Kings 11:4).
  - ◦ David was blind to his own sin until he was rebuked by Nathan the prophet (2 Kings 12:1–7).
  - ◦ Consequences of David's selfishness: adultery, murder of Uriah, death of his son by Bathsheba, ongoing strife and sedition in his own family, public exposure of his sin (2 Kings 12:10–12).
- James and John (disciples of Jesus) (Matt. 20:20–28)
  - ◦ James and John wanted positions of honor, power, and prestige in the Messiah's kingdom.
  - ◦ They exhibited an attitude of entitlement; after all, they left Papa Zebedee and a lucrative fishing business.
  - ◦ They convinced their mother to put the case before Jesus. (Selfishness will use anyone to achieve the desired ends.)
  - ◦ James and John showed no concern for the others or the other disciple's positions in kingdom.
  - ◦ James and John were willing to be alienated from the others to get what they wanted.
  - ◦ Consequences of selfish desire for position: alienation from the group. The ten remaining disciples were very angry when they heard what James and John had done.
- Jesus' response to their request:
  - ◦ Talked about suffering, not honor or prestige.
  - ◦ Positions of honor were given by the Father, not Jesus.

- Taught: if you would be great, be a servant to all.
  "But Jesus called them to Himself and said, 'You know that the rulers of the Gentiles lord it over them, and those who are great exercise authority over them. Yet it shall not be so among you; but whoever desires to become great among you, let him be your servant. And whoever desires to be first among you, let him be your slave—just as the Son of Man did not come to be served, but to serve, and to give His life a ransom for many'" (Matt. 20:26–28 NKJV).

- Both brothers in the parable of the prodigal son (Luke 15:11–32)
  - The younger brother: selfishly wanted his inheritance *now!*
    - He wanted to spend the money as he saw fit (entitlement).
    - In effect, he was saying to the father, "You are as dead to me."
    - Showed no concern for the father's feelings or for his estate.
    - Wasted what the father gave him in riotous living.
    - Consequences: he quickly came to poverty and want.
  - The Older brother (self-righteous attitude): angry that the brother was so well received after what he had done.
    - Angry response: cites his own good works (Luke 15: 29).
    - No compassion for repentant brother who was in dire need (Luke 15:30).
    - Modern psychologists define selfishness as "lack of empathy."
  - Consequences: relationships in the family were strained.

Selfless examples—recognizing the difference: In the following examples, try to identify the attitude toward self, the unselfish action, and the consequences of unselfish action.

- Abraham (Gen. 13:1–12)
  - Lot, Abraham's nephew, prospered as Abraham prospered.
  - Both had flocks and herds in abundance, so that the land could not support both.
  - Strife ensued between the herdsmen of Lot and herdsmen of Abraham.
    - Explore Abraham's selfless attitude: he offered Lot first choice of land to settle in.
    - Abraham had a right to choose first as the elder, and the head of the clan.
    - Examine Lot's selfish attitude: he did not yield to Uncle Abraham but accepted first choice without argument, choosing the very best for himself. (Gen.13:11).
  - Consequences of selfless choice vs. selfish choice: Abraham was blessed; while Lot lost it all (Gen. 14:1–12)
- Joseph (Gen. 45:2–24)
  - He had a "right" to be angry with brothers who sold him into slavery.
  - He had power to seek retribution for wrongs done to him.
  - Joseph had an attitude of forgiveness and love for his brothers.
  - Joseph had a right view of himself (Gen. 45:5–8) as God's servant.
  - Unselfish action; he provided for them and gave them the best of the land.
  - Consequences: re-united with father and brothers.
- The Samaritan in the parable of the Good Samaritan (Luke 10:30–37)
  - Unselfish action showed his attitude of compassion.
  - Outwardly pious priest and Levite were a contrast; no empathy.
  - Samaritan used his own resources to help a stranger from a sometimes hostile nation.

- Consequences of his action: he served as contrast, and we are still talking about him after two millennia.
- Barnabas (Acts 4:36)
  - Responded to the need of the Christians in Jerusalem by selling his land and giving the proceeds to the apostles.
  - Barnabas was a Levite (could have considered himself more important that the apostles (fishermen).
  - Consequences: called "son of encouragement" by the apostles; good reputation among the saints.
- Paul (Gal. 2:20)
  - He was an "up-and-comer" in the Jewish religious community.
  - Well educated, well respected, given authority to eradicate the believers in Jesus.
  - When called by Jesus, Saul of Tarsus gave up everything to become Paul, the apostle of Jesus Christ.
  - He sacrificed reputation, career, finances, safety, in order to preach salvation to the Gentiles (Gal. 2:20).
  - Paul's view of self: dead to the flesh, alive in Christ.
  - Paul said he had given control of his life over to Christ and became obedient to Jesus in all things.
- Jesus (Phil. 2:1–11)
  - Jesus's attitude of selflessness:
    "Let this mind be in you, which was also in Christ Jesus: Who, being in the form of God, thought it not robbery to be equal with God: But made himself of no reputation, and took upon him the form of a servant, and was made in the likeness of men" (Phil. 2:5–7).
  - Jesus's unselfish action: "And being found in fashion as a man, he humbled himself, and became obedient unto death, even the death of the cross" (Phil. 2:8).
  - Consequences: "Wherefore God also hath highly exalted him, and given him a name which is above every name: That at the name of Jesus every knee should bow, of things in heaven, and things in earth, and things under the earth;

And that every tongue should confess that Jesus Christ is Lord, to the glory of God the Father" (Phil. 2:9–11).

- How should we conduct ourselves?
  - Paul charges us to consider ourselves as dead to sin; including selfishness "Likewise reckon ye also yourselves to be dead indeed unto sin, but alive unto God through Jesus Christ our Lord" (Rom. 6:11).
  - Putting self to death is accomplished by:
  - Self-denial. Humbling yourself before God and esteeming others better than yourself (Matt. 16:24; Luke 9:23).
  - Self-control. Bringing every thought and action into conformity with the will of God (Prov. 16:32; Gal. 5:23; 2 Peter 1:6).
  - Self-sacrifice (2 Cor. 8:5; Rom. 12:1–2). Christians are to be "living sacrifices" unto God, living each day to accomplish the good works for which they were created so that Father and Son might be glorified.

What Is the Biblical Cause of Low Self-Esteem?
- Why God Created You.
  - To have dominion over His earthly creation
  - To have fellowship with God; garden experience (1 Cor. 1:9)
  - To be fruitful and fill the earth (Gen. 1:28)
  - To love God and be obedient to Him (Eccl. 12:13)
  - To serve Him faithfully (1 Sam. 12:24)
  - To do good works (Eph. 2:10)
  - To love God and to love each other (Matt. 22:37–35)
- The Origin of Low Self-Esteem
  And when the woman saw that the tree was good for food, and that it was pleasant to the eyes, and a tree to be desired to make one wise, she took of the fruit thereof, and did eat, and gave also unto her husband with her; and he did eat. And the eyes of them both were opened, and they knew that they were naked; and they sewed fig leaves together, and made themselves aprons. And they heard the voice of the LORD God walking in the garden in the cool of the day: and Adam and his wife hid

themselves from the presence of the LORD God amongst the trees of the garden. And the LORD God called unto Adam, and said unto him, where art thou? And he said, I heard thy voice in the garden, and I was afraid, because I was naked; and I hid myself. (Gen. 3:1–10)

- ◦ When Adam sinned, shame and guilt entered in, and they hid from God.
- ◦ Low self-esteem is a result of missing the mark
- ◦ The Bible calls this *sin*.
- ◦ Because of sin, we are no longer able to fulfill our purpose before God.
- ◦ God's plan of salvation *restores* us.

How the Self-Esteem Builders Have Damaged the Church

- • Working to improve self-esteem negates salvation based on the grace of God.
  - ◦ Working to improve what you think about yourself blocks the light of truth.
  - ◦ "And this is the condemnation, that light is come into the world, and men loved darkness rather than light, because their deeds were evil" (John 3:19).
  - ◦ Our relationship with God is not based on our own righteousness but upon His grace.
    "But when the kindness and the love of God our Savior toward man appeared, not by works of righteousness which we have done, but according to His mercy He saved us, through the washing of regeneration and renewing of the Holy Spirit, whom He poured out on us abundantly through Jesus Christ our Savior, that having been justified by His grace we should become heirs according to the hope of eternal life" (Titus 3:4–7 NKJV).
    "But God commends his love toward us, in that, while we were yet sinners, Christ died for us" (Rom. 5:8).
  - ◦ I do wrong because I have a sin nature, not because of low self-esteem.

Churches are damaged when they refuse to preach about sin.

- Calling an action a sin is regarded as an act of bigotry, judgment, and hatred.
- Christians must stand on the truth of God's Word that men have sinned and that there are certain activities that God considers sin.
  - Paul tells us: "For all have sinned, and come short of the glory of God" (Rom. 3:23).
- Acknowledging sin does not damage self-esteem but is the first step in getting free of shame and guilt.
- Recognizing sin does not set an individual up for condemnation but opens the door for the mercy and grace of God to be received (Rom. 7 and 8).
- Christ came into the world to save sinners. So when people say that what they do is not sin, they close the door for Christ to show them His love, grace, compassion, and peace.

Churches are damaged when self-improvement programs replace the work of the Holy Spirit.

- The emphasis is on the works of the individual, rather than the work of God.
- Worldly remedies for poor self-esteem. Example: "Look into yourself."
- Satan is the source of this "remedy" for low self-esteem.
  "Ye shall be as gods. For God doth know that in the day ye eat thereof, then your eyes shall be opened, and ye shall be as gods, knowing good and evil" (Gen 3:5).
  - This kind of self-esteem (being as God) leads to independent feelings and self-sufficiency.
  - Trust in one's own ability to overcome is not of faith and therefore is also *sin*.
- The work of the Holy Spirit is to convict of sin and righteousness and to teach us.
- Power over sin comes from God's grace (Rom. 6:14).

Churches are reluctant to teach about coming judgment and hell.

- Paul spoke to his followers about the content of his preaching: "For I have not shunned to declare unto you all the counsel of God" (Acts 20:27).
- Judgment and hell are part of the whole counsel of God and must be taught.
- Any "fix" outside of God is faulty, incomplete and, at best, temporary.
  - The self-image improvement movement is neither biblical nor scientific.
  - We can *and must* choose to live by the infallible, never-changing Word of God!

Signs of the end times
- In the last days, people will not accept sound doctrine.
  "For the time will come when they will not endure sound doctrine; but after their own lusts shall they heap to themselves teachers, having itching ears; and they shall turn away their ears from the truth, and shall be turned unto fables" (2 Tim. 4:3–4).
- What "itching ears" want to hear.
  - People today do not want to hear about sin, death, judgment, and hell.
  - Tell me how blessed I am; how I can increase in wealth and influence.
  - Tell me about love and the wonderful plan God has for my life.
  - Consider the teaching in "mega-churches"; few teach the whole counsel of God.

How should a Christian view the problem of low self-esteem?
- Key question: what is the source of my self-esteem?
- "God resisteth the proud, but giveth grace unto the humble" (James 4:6).
- Being humble does not mean Christians should have low self-esteem, but the source of our self-esteem is critical.

- If we trust in earthly resources (including ourselves), we will inevitably be left with a sense of worth rooted in pride. (Look what I did!)
- Jesus said: "So likewise ye, when ye shall have done all those things which are commanded you, say, We are *unprofitable servants*: we have done that which was *our duty to do*" (Luke 17:10, emphasis added) So much for pride!
- Our sense of well-being should not depend on what we do but on who we are in Christ.
  - Sorry, folks, there is no good thing in us. Apostle Paul wrote about himself:
  - "For I know that in me (that is, in my flesh,) dwelleth no good thing: for to will is present with me; but how to perform that which is good I find not" (Rom. 7:18).
  - No good thing inside. Jesus said, "For from within, out of the heart of men, proceed evil thoughts, adulteries, fornications, murders, Thefts, covetousness, wickedness, deceit, lasciviousness, an evil eye, blasphemy, pride, foolishness: All these evil things come from within, and defile the man" (Mark 7:21–23).
  - So much for looking within yourself to build self-esteem.
- Christian's Self-Worth Comes from Having a Right Relationship with God.
- We know our value to God because of the price He paid for us through the blood of Jesus Christ. "For ye are bought with a price: therefore glorify God in your body, and in your spirit, which are God's" (1 Cor. 6:20).
- Recognize Your Value to God. You *Are* Special—Here Is Why!
  - You are individually chosen.
  - God chooses "the nots." You are chosen because you are a "not," not because of talent, looks, actions, etc.
    "But God hath chosen the foolish things of the world to confound the wise; and God hath chosen the weak things of the world to confound the things which are mighty; And base things of the world, and things which are despised,

hath God chosen, yea, and things which are not, to bring to nought things that are" (1 Cor.7:27–28).

- ○ God knew you and chose you from the foundation of the world. (You are special because of God, not because of you!) Blessed be the God and Father of our Lord Jesus Christ, who hath blessed us with all spiritual blessings in heavenly places in Christ: According as he hath chosen us in him before the foundation of the world, that we should be holy and without blame before him in love: Having predestinated us unto the adoption of children by Jesus Christ to himself, according to the good pleasure of his will, To the praise of the glory of his grace, wherein he hath made us accepted in the beloved In whom we have redemption through his blood, the forgiveness of sins, according to the riches of his grace. (Eph. 1:3–7)

- ○ Any kudos (praise for achievement, etc.) is meant to glorify God, not you. You are a chosen vehicle to show forth His glory. (You are special because of this.) "But ye are a chosen generation, a royal priesthood, an holy nation, a peculiar people; that ye should shew forth the praises of him who hath called you out of darkness into his marvellous light" (1 Peter 2:9).

- You are the Father's gift to His Son, Jesus
"And this is the Father's will which hath sent me, that of all which He hath given me I should lose nothing, but should raise it up again at the last day" (John 6:39).

- Jesus prayed for you in Gethsemane. "I pray for them: I pray not for the world, but for them which thou hast given me; for they are thine ... And now I am no more in the world, but these are in the world, and I come to thee. Holy Father, keep through thine own name those whom thou hast given me, that they may be one, as we are" (John 17:9, 11).

- You will be with Jesus for eternity to see His glory. "Father, I will that they also, whom thou hast given me, be with me where I am; that they may behold my glory, which thou hast given me: for thou lovedst me before the foundation of the world" (John 17:24).

- Jesus continues to intercede for you. You are never alone. Jesus has not gone back to heaven to take a little coffee break but continues His work, interceding for you against the accusations of the Evil One (Rom. 8:34; Heb. 7:25).

CHAPTER TWO

The Truth about Consequences

Bob, our Christian stand-in, recognized there were stumbling blocks in his life that kept him from being effective in the kingdom of God. He knew his lack of preparedness and feelings of inadequacy were the cause of his failure to spread the gospel of Jesus Christ. However, stumbling blocks are the product of multiple causes. Good preparation means digging a little deeper, often exposing our emotions as the probable culprit. For Bob to be fully prepared, he must do more than study. He must confront feelings of guilt, anger, jealousy, greed, and the specter of fear. Operating out of emotional hurt can cloud your motives and your ministry and severely limit success in personal outreach. Many good books are available that deal with emotions, and it would be a good move to study one of them in your effort to prepare yourself for kingdom service.

Groundwork

Although emotional healing is not our principal focus, fear is something we will address from time to time. Fear is a prime weapon utilized by the Enemy to keep a Christian soldier immobilized, and our mission is to invade enemy territory and take spoils. Fear is natural but must be confronted and overcome if we are to succeed. Before Joshua went forward to battle, the Lord spoke to him.

> Only be thou strong and very courageous, that thou
> mayest observe to do according to all the law, which
> Moses my servant commanded thee: turn not from it
> to the right handor to the left, that thou mayest prosper
> withersoever thou goest. (Josh. 1:7)

Even mighty general Joshua had to confront his fear and do a heart check, fixing his eyes upon the written Word of God and the mission the Lord gave him. We cannot expect to do less.

Fear can be diffused at the outset if we realize that the victory has already been won for us. Joshua's mission was to destroy the Canaanites and take the land, but it was not a cakewalk. Battles needed to be fought, and lessons had to be learned. The outcome was guaranteed as long as everything was done the Lord's way. Jericho fell miraculously, but Ai was a different story. One of Joshua's troopers, Aachen, the son of Carmi, could not resist helping himself to some silver and gold and a fancy suit of clothes from the spoils of Jericho, ignoring the Lord's edict that all the spoils of Jericho were to be considered accursed. Because of just one man's greed, the battle was lost, and thirty-six warriors died. The entire invading force was unable to achieve victory because one man stepped out from under the covering of the Lord. The impact to Israel went beyond the obvious sadness incurred through loss. Fear and bewilderment dwelt in their tents; and even gripped the heart of their commander.

> And Joshua rent his clothes, and fell to the earth upon
> his face before the ark of the LORD until the eventide,
> he and the elders of Israel, and put dust upon their heads.
> And Joshua said, Alas, O Lord GOD, wherefore hast
> thou at all brought this people over Jordan, to deliver us
> into the hand of the Amorites, to destroy us? Would to
> God we had been content, and dwelt on the other side
> Jordan! O Lord, what shall I say, when Israel turneth
> their backs before their enemies! (Josh. 7:6–8)

In response to Joshua's prayer, the Lord helped them identify the root of failure and rectify the problem. When Israel was again blameless before Him and the fear of another defeat was overcome, the Lord provided Joshua with a new plan and a promise of victory over Ai (Josh. 8:1).

It is a great comfort for us to know that, like Joshua, we already have the victory through Jesus Christ and that we can overcome our flesh and the works of the Enemy. Operating from a position of victory is the chief dynamic in overcoming fear. However, we cannot get sloppy in either preparation or performance. The apostle Peter warned us to be both sober and vigilant, for, like Aachen, we can allow the Enemy to gain access and bring defeat (1 Peter 5:8). We need to enter into the battle, but God has already determined victory if we keep our eyes on Him.

Preparing for Battle

Overcoming fear requires a daily self-evaluation. Before a young King David went into battle, he did a heart check. He did not trust his own assessment but asked for God's illumination of any imperfection that would impede victory.

"Search me, O God, and know my heart: try me, and know my thoughts: And see if there be any wicked way in me, and lead me in the way everlasting" (Ps. 139:23–24).

When there was sin, he confessed it and received forgiveness, knowing this was a necessity for continuing on successfully in the service of God (Ps. 51). David knew he needed to be in right relationship with the Lord in order to expect victory. He fought many battles, and before David went to war, his heart was fixed and his mouth was filled with praise. "My heart is fixed, O God, my heart is fixed: I will sing and give praise" (Ps. 57:7). David knew exactly what he would do when confronted with a challenge. Once we have examined our hearts and received the Lord's cleansing of sin, our hearts must also become fixed on the task at hand. Fixing our hearts on the task at hand means examining and clearly identifying our motive for evangelism.

Conquerors Reach Out

Satan is a master strategist and would like nothing better than to keep Christian soldiers selfishly consumed with their own well-being. Our assignment is to make disciples of all nations. We are called "more than conquerors," but conquerors don't sit home in the comfort of their own church, sucking up the good things all the time. They must reach out. Entire churches have fallen into the Enemy's trap, focusing only on growing their own congregations. We cannot fulfill the Lord's command and still remain card-carrying members of the Me generation. This is not what we are called to do. I do not want to be among those that will have to answer the Lord's question, "Why call ye me, Lord, Lord, and do not the things I say?" (Luke 6:46).

Jesus told a parable about a nobleman who delivered his goods to his servants with the instruction to "occupy till I come." "Occupy" is a military term. Conquerors are to "occupy"; that is, take care of business and reach out to extend the influence of the kingdom of God. If we are to be successful in our mission, we must become of one mind with the Lord and spread His ways and His Word wherever we go. Why we reach out is vital.

If you are striving to extend your own influence and authority, you are headed for disaster. There is only one true motive for outreach, and that motive is love. We reach out because we love the Lord, and He has asked us to do it. We reach out because we are of one mind with God, who loved the world enough to send His own Son to die for the redemption of many. Once we get a picture of the consequences of not having a relationship with the Lord, our motivation level increases drastically. This is why we *activate* and allow all the love poured into us to overflow to others.

Lord, Open My Eyes to the Lost!

I was thirty-five years old before I came to know the Lord Jesus in a personal way. Before that day, I did not know I was lost. This is a common condition found in those who have been raised in a "nice" family. I intellectually believed in Jesus and His resurrection, and I subscribed to all the rituals required by my parents' church. Since I was now a church member in good standing, I reasoned that I must therefore be a Christian. The sad fact is I was lost and did not have a clue as to my real spiritual condition. There was a time in my life when I stopped clinging to the socially acceptable mores of my parents and fell into deep sin. It may sound strange, but that was the best thing that could have happened to me. Clearly, I had no power over the sin in my life, and I could not deny I desperately needed a savior. For the unsaved, when things are going well in their lives, the chance of realizing their true condition is more remote. Like the church of Laodicea described by Jesus, we think we are "rich, and increased with goods, and have need of nothing," but we really are "wretched, and miserable, and poor, and blind, and naked" (Rev 3:17). Many people in our sphere of influence who are not in covenant with the Lord don't know they need to be in such a relationship until trouble comes their way.

First Attempts

My first experience in street ministry was in New York City. I worked with a seasoned minister in Midtown Manhattan at Rockefeller Center. The people who walked these streets were, for the most part, businessmen and businesswomen, carrying their briefcases and dressed in upscale office attire. The atmosphere was hard and cold. Virtually none of these folks was open to hearing about his or her need for a savior; all were engaged in climbing the corporate ladder. Few people were even willing to accept a gospel tract, and if they did, they disposed of it in the wastebasket on the corner. For them, the need for a savior was not relative.

Shortly after that time, I worked with a different group closer to Times Square. (This was before urban rejuvenation transformed Times Square from "hooker heaven" to a more commercially productive area.) Unlike the people at Rockefeller Center, the people walking the streets surrounding Times Square knew they were in sin. Drug users, homeless folks, alcoholics, and prostitutes did not need to be told they had spiritual problems. They were more open to hearing God's plan for redemption because they saw their personal needs. They were lost, and they knew it. Contrasting these two locales showed me that before the gospel becomes meat, there must be a hunger. Jesus said it this way:

"They that be whole need not a physician, but they that are sick. But go ye and learn what that meaneth, I will have mercy, and not sacrifice: for I am not come to call the righteous, but sinners to repentance" (Matt. 9:12–13).

In Case You Don't Remember

An advantage to being thirty-five at the time of salvation is that I clearly remember many of the thirty-four years of sinful living that preceded the glorious event. In case you grew up under the fourth pew at church and don't remember (or never knew) what serious sin and separation from God was like, I will include these observations common to the unsaved. Regardless of the social strata, there is a nagging feeling of emptiness in life. It just does not make sense, but it is most certainly present; something is definitely missing, though it is not easily defined. Even if the externals of life seem to be going well and they have a degree of prosperity, there is still that irksome void. There is no peace, but most don't know why. If life is not going well, they blame the void on whatever they perceive is missing. "If only I had a good job, or a good spouse; or a better home, or I could kick this habit, then I would know peace." In order to remedy the uncomfortable nagging, they chase after their own form of "fix." Maybe it is wealth, power, prestige, expensive toys, or good times, all of which have no eternal value. If and when they succeed in their pursuit and those externals are added to their lives, the relief is only temporary. There is still no satisfaction in the inner man, and so the chase is on again, with an increased intensity for more of the same or "bigger and better." Some will never achieve to the degree they believe they should, and they mistakenly identify the root cause of their emptiness as failure to achieve goals instead of sin. They look elsewhere for an explanation of the nagging void. Blame is assigned to everything from the economic conditions of birth to the undeserved poor marks given to them by their third-grade teacher. No matter the contrived explanation of perceived failure, it is not the true cause of discomfort. Sin has separated them from God, and that is a very empty place to be indeed. Worldly success will never quench that empty feeling. Think about the number of rich and famous people who end their own lives because there is no peace.

Numbing the Hurt

Trying to pursue happiness without Jesus is not only fruitless, but it is downright painful. Some choose a form of self-medication, like alcohol, drugs, sex, entertainment, excess devotion to work—anything to keep that feeling at bay, but it will never be satiated until the cause is satisfied. I spent a few years well medicated with alcohol, trying to numb the hurt and empty feelings that brought me to thoughts of suicide on more than one occasion. I had no power over the sin in my life. This is what it feels like to be lost. Before I was saved by God's grace, I enjoyed worldly success, financial comfort, and a degree of popularity, certainly to a much greater degree than I do at present. However, I would not trade one minute of the peace that Jesus has given me for all the success this world has to offer. I know what it means to be without hope in this life. When Jesus entered my life, I asked Him to never let me forget what life was like without Him. Remembering the intense pain of emptiness is an "activator" for me.

And If That Is Not Enough

The truth about the consequences of leaving this planet without a relationship with Jesus Christ is enough to activate you into motion. The burden of getting someone saved is not on your shoulders, but we are the tools the Lord uses to make His plan of salvation known. Recently I saw a photo taken in the city of Mecca in Saudi Arabia. In the center of the photo was a black shrine surrounded by so many figures dressed in white, they were indistinguishable as individuals. These deluded souls were performing a ritual pilgrimage required by the religion of Islam. There were so many people surrounding the shrine, the area appeared to be snow-covered, until I remembered it was located in Saudi Arabia. It took a little while for me to realize that each of these white blips was a person who is lost. Despite the fact these folks have become sworn enemies of both Jews and Christians, it broke my heart that they were exercising such diligence while galloping down the path to hell. If this does not move you, perhaps you have overlooked what Jesus told us about hell.

In our sophisticated culture, there are many who have chosen not to believe in the existence of hell. We have trivialized it, making the very word part of our everyday four-letter vocabulary. Churches have ignored and avoided teaching about hell because the picture of Jesus they have chosen to project does not include any negativity at all. This is not a valid representation, because a God of mercy must also be a God of justice. Justice requires judgment, and judgment for the lost includes a very extreme negative outcome. For me, if it is in the Bible, then who am I to say it doesn't exist? Jesus is the major source of the information we have about hell, and He spoke more about that place than He did about heaven.

Old Testament believers were not acquainted with hell in the same way as the contemporaries of Jesus. They simply knew that death was, for the most part, inevitable and that afterward, they would go to *sheol*, the place where the dead congregated. The prophet Daniel spoke of a resurrection from the grave to be followed by judgment. The concept that something would occur after death was not entirely foreign to believers before the time of Jesus (Dan.12:2). They obviously were not overtaken by surprise at His teaching.

Jesus warned about the terrible consequences of hell in a most graphic picture.

> And if thy hand offend thee, cut it off: it is better for thee to enter into life maimed, than having two hands to go into hell, into the fire that never shall be quenched: Where their worm dieth not, and the fire is not quenched. And if thy foot offend thee, cut it off: it is better for thee to enter halt into life, than having two feet to be cast into hell, into the fire that never shall be

quenched: Where their worm dieth not, and the fire is not quenched. And if thine eye offend thee, pluck it out: it is better for thee to enter into the kingdom of God with one eye, than having two eyes to be cast into hell fire: Where their worm dieth not, and the fire is not quenched. (Mark 9:42–48)

Of course, the emphasis was on the extremely drastic penalty of hellfire that would not be quenched, not on self-mutilation. Jesus contrasted a temporary condition with the eternal consequences.

Jesus provided other descriptions of the afterlife dwelling place of the lost. He related an account of a rich man and a beggar that some call a fictitious parable, while others believe it is an actual event. No matter which position you favor, Jesus did not provide details that were untrue or confusing.

There was a certain rich man, which was clothed in purple and fine linen, and fared sumptuously every day: And there was a certain beggar named Lazarus, which was laid at his gate, full of sores, And desiring to be fed with the crumbs which fell from the rich man's table: moreover the dogs came and licked his sores.

And it came to pass, that the beggar died, and was carried by the angels into Abraham's bosom: the rich man also died, and was buried; And in hell he lift up his eyes, being in torments, and seeth Abraham afar off, and Lazarus in his bosom. And he cried and said, Father Abraham, have mercy on me, and send Lazarus, that he may dip the tip of his finger in water, and cool my tongue; for I am tormented in this flame. But Abraham said, Son, remember that thou in thy lifetime receivedst thy good things, and likewise Lazarus evil things: but now he is comforted, and thou art tormented. And beside all this, between us and you there is a great gulf fixed: so that they which would pass from hence to you cannot; neither can they pass to us that would come from thence.

Then he said, I pray thee therefore, father, that thou wouldest send him to my father's house: For I have five brethren; that he may testify unto them, lest they also come into this place of torment. Abraham saith unto him They have Moses and the prophets; let them hear them. And he said, Nay, father Abraham: but if one went unto them from the dead, they will repent. And he said unto him, If they hear not Moses and the prophets, neither will they be persuaded, though one rose from the dead. (Luke 16:19–31)

Jesus described a holding place for the dead, divided into two sections. One section was called "Abraham's bosom," a place of comfort, where the righteous dead waited, and another section was called "Torments." Here, the lost were held, awaiting final judgment. The word "torment" can refer to both great bodily pain and mental pain, and the suffering of the rich man certainly reflects both. He experienced extreme thirst, brought about by flames and the hopelessness that this was to be his eternal state. Hopelessness was paired with helplessness, as there was nothing he could do to warn his family of the reality of the torment that awaited them.

Hell's Population Count

The disciples asked Jesus if there were many who were saved. He answered, "Enter ye in at the strait gate: for wide is the gate, and broad is the way, that leadeth to destruction, and many there be which go in there at: Because strait is the gate, and narrow is the way, which leadeth unto life, and few there be that find it" (Matt.7:13–14).

The lost, like the brothers of the rich man, need to hear the truth now, and the consequences of an eternity in hell is a great activator.

Bringing the Mission Field to Your Doorstep

Right now you may be thinking of a loved one who is not in a relationship with Jesus Christ. Your heart's desire is to see him/her come to know the peace of Jesus Christ. Your heart is motivated to reach out to him/her, but you wonder how you can do this. Perhaps you have no specific person in mind but you love Jesus and want to bring others to Him. What is the next step after your heart has been set in motion?

Study/Teaching Outline: The Truth about Consequences

More than a Conqueror—Removing Stumbling Blocks
- Identifying stumbling blocks that hinder effectiveness in the kingdom of God
- Overcoming feelings of unpreparedness and inadequacy
- Taking authority over your emotions
  - Emotional healing—confronting feelings of guilt, anger, jealousy, greed
  - Operating out of hurt can cloud your ministry.
  - Do a daily heart checkup so that the Enemy doesn't regain ground.
- Becoming "more than a conqueror" and confronting fear.
- Fear and the list of things over which we are conquerors (Romans 8:35–37).
  - Trouble, hardship, persecution, lack, danger, and our flesh
  - Fear will immobilize a conqueror.
  - Conquerors must confront fear (Josh. 1:7).
  - Conquerors must be submitted to the Lord (Josh. 7 and 8).
  - The Lord helps us identify and rectify problem areas.
- What do conquerors do? Conquerors reach out and conquer the works of the Enemy.
- The Enemy wants us to stay consumed with ourselves.

Preparing for Battle
- Stay clean before the Lord (Ps. 139:23–24; Ps. 51).
- Lean not to your own understanding (Prov. 3:5–7).
- Accept the Lord's correction and submit to His discipline (Prov. 3:11–13).
- Fix your heart on the Lord (Ps. 57:7).
- Become one of God's occupation troops.

Opening Your Eyes to the Lost. What does it mean to be lost?
- Having a huge hole in the heart.
- What we know that non-Christians don't know about themselves is that they have a hole in them that only God can fill.
- They are miserable without God and don't know the reason for their emptiness.
- They chase after empty things like wealth, power, and prestige that have no eternal value. In the end, they will still die and face God's judgment.
    ◦ Some drown their misery in alcohol, drugs, sex, food, television, and the acquisition of things.
    ◦ Nothing will satisfy, long term, except a relationship with Jesus Christ.
- True condition of the lost: they are God's enemy, no matter how nice they seem to be.
- Without a relationship with Jesus, they are a friend of the world and an enemy of God (James 4:4).
- Acquire the right motive for outreach—love for the Lord and others
- What is the heart activator for you?

Leaving This Life without a Covenant with Jesus
- Death is inevitable. "And as it is appointed unto men once to die, but after this the judgment" (Heb. 9:27). Only one generation will escape death through the rapture, and all those will be believers in Jesus Christ.
- The ultimate eternal destiny of those who die without Jesus is called the Lake of Fire (Rev. 20:15).

- The immediate holding place of those who die without Christ is called hell, and almost all of the information we have about hell comes from the teachings of Jesus.
- Jesus talked more about hell than He did about heaven. Some examples:
  - A place of unquenchable fire
    And if thy hand offend thee, cut it off: it is better for thee to enter into life maimed, than having two hands to go into hell, into the fire that never shall be quenched: Where their worm dieth not, and the fire is not quenched. And if thy foot offend thee, cut it off: it is better for thee to enter halt into life, than having two feet to be cast into hell, into the fire that never shall be quenched: Where their worm dieth not, and the fire is not quenched. And if thine eye offend thee, pluck it out: it is better for thee to enter into the kingdom of God with one eye, than having two eyes to be cast into hell fire: Where their worm dieth not, and the fire is not quenched. (Mark 9:43–48)
    - ✓ *Note: This does not mean to go out and mutilate yourself.
  - Many will choose to go to hell.
    "For wide is the gate and broad is the road that leads to destruction, and many enter through it. But small is the gate and narrow the road that leads to life, and only a few find it" (Matt. 5:22).
  - General description: Jesus tells us more in the Gospels. He describes the "weeping and gnashing of teeth," the "eternal fire," the "outer darkness," the "worm [that] does not die, and the fire that is not quenched."
  - Eternal nature of Lake of Fire. He also makes it clear that hell, and subsequently the Lake of Fire, is not temporary but eternal.
- The parable of Lazarus and the rich man:
  There was a rich man who was dressed in purple and fine linen and lived in luxury every day. At his gate was laid a beggar named Lazarus, covered with sores and longing to eat what

37

fell from the rich man's table. Even the dogs came and licked his sores. The time came when the beggar died and the angels carried him to Abraham's side.

- ◦ This was at the paradise section. Before Jesus died, no one could enter into heaven.
- ◦ Jesus pictures a chamber divided into two sections.
- ◦ The righteous dead were separated from the wicked dead.
- ◦ God always made a difference between the holy and the profane (Lev. 10:10).
- ◦ The place of the wicked dead, called Torments, was a place of suffering, both physical (heat) and mental (hopelessness, helplessness).

The rich man also died and was buried. In Hades [hell], where he was in torment, he looked up and saw Abraham far away, with Lazarus by his side. So he called to him, "Father Abraham, have pity on me and send Lazarus to dip the tip of his finger in water and cool my tongue, because I am in agony in this fire." But Abraham replied, "Son, remember that in your lifetime you received your good things, while Lazarus received bad things, but now he is comforted here and you are in agony. And besides all this, between us and you a great chasm has been set in place, so that those who want to go from here to you cannot, nor can anyone cross over from there to us."

He answered, "Then I beg you, father, send Lazarus to my family, for I have five brothers. Let him warn them, so that they will not also come to this place of torment." Abraham replied, "They have Moses and the Prophets; let them listen to them." "No, father Abraham," he said, "but if someone from the dead goes to them, they will repent." He said to them, "If they do not listen to Moses and the Prophets, they will not be convinced if someone rises from the dead." (Luke 16:19–31)

- ◦ Conclusion after considering the condition of the lost. The "lost" need to hear the truth *now*, while they are alive.

Bringing the Mission Field to Your Doorstep
- The lost are all around you.
  Are there many who are saved? Strait gate for narrow is the way (Matt. 7:13–14).
- Mission field is vast—"all the world"
- Not everyone is called to go on the foreign mission field.
- Our mission field is close to home, on our own doorsteps.
- Contrast our privileged position; what it means to be saved.
- Benefits of our covenant relationship
  "We are confident, I say, and willing rather to be absent from the body, and to be present with the Lord" (2 Cor. 5:8). In other words, when we pass from this life, in an instant, we will be present with God in heaven.
- Think about your family, friends, and acquaintances who are unsaved. Recognizing their lost condition and eternal destiny is strong motivation to activate your heart and do all you can to help them enter the kingdom of God.
- Seeking God for your prayer assignment
  ○ Prayer assignment: Ask the Lord who He is leading you to target in prayer for salvation.
  ○ Focus on that person and make him/her your assignment in prayer.

CHAPTER THREE

God Does All the Heavy Lifting

We can categorize people in many different ways. We can group them by language, gender, race, country of origin, and so on, but as far as God is concerned, there are only two possible categories: those who have a redemptive covenant sealed with the blood of Jesus Christ, and those who do not. Since the birth of the church two thousand years ago, many denominations have sprung up under the banner of Christianity. They disagree on many things, but those that are truly Christian agree on at least two major issues. In every field of study and in every worldview, there will be some disagreement. We may disagree on lesser issues, but the core doctrines of Christianity are constant from denomination to denomination. One such cardinal truth is that Jesus is the only way to salvation. Scripture testifies to this truth in John 14:6, Acts 4:12, and Romans 6:23. Holding to this gospel truth alone will cause you to be hated by the world. Christians are called elitists, exclusionary, ignorant, and provincial. Those are the socially polite names applied, and I'm sure you've heard Christians tagged with additional and far less printable names. Nevertheless, the truth is clearly given to us in the written Word of God.

If we are to reach out to the lost in the name of Jesus, we need to have a basic doctrinal understanding about our God, what is a real Christian, and how people get saved. If we are to reach out and repeat Jesus's invitation to come unto Him, we need to have some understanding of who He is. The identity and nature of Jesus Christ is a cardinal doctrine of the church. The purpose of this study is to activate you for witnessing, not to add to the many excellent doctrinal books available, so this chapter will be very basic indeed. Do not become concerned that you need a theological degree in order to witness. Some of you, however, may be experiencing a strong desire to skip this chapter because studying doctrine is not to your taste. When I was growing up, I did not like vegetables, especially carrots. Mom insisted that I needed vegetables to grow strong—and carrots, in particular, so that I would develop sharp vision. "Eat all those carrots!" That was an order from Mom. Believer, you need to eat your carrots too! You may think studying doctrine is distasteful, but doctrine is necessary for you to have sharp vision into spiritual things. The carrots in this chapter are fresh and sweet and will strengthen your ability to fulfill the Lord's command. A believer is used as a tool of the Lord in the salvation process. You, by yourself, cannot save an insect. People are saved by the power of God; therefore, you can relax. God does all the heavy lifting.

What Is God Like?

One of the joys of both this life and the next is discovering wonderful things about the God we serve. We will never know all there is about Him, but we can begin our quest to learn with some basics from the Bible The Bible has come to us through the work and life blood of many individuals, and since God has gone to such great lengths to reveal Himself, it is our job to learn as much as we can from His written Word.

"Seek the LORD and his strength, seek his face continually" (1 Chron. 16:11).

Those of us who diligently seek Him are promised a great reward. We shall indeed find Him, and we shall be given understanding.

"For I know the thoughts that I think toward you, saith the LORD, thoughts of peace, and not of evil, to give you an expected end. Then shall ye call upon me, and ye shall go and pray unto me, and I will hearken unto you. And ye shall seek me, and find me, when ye shall search for me with all your heart" (Jer. 29:11–13).

"Evil men understand not judgment: but they that seek the LORD understand all things" (Prov. 28:5).

The first exciting thing we can conclude from Scripture is that God wants to be known. Since Moses first sat down next to a bowl of manna chips to write the Pentateuch, the Lord has revealed Himself progressively. His nature was revealed in various names such as, "El Shaddai" (God Almighty) in Genesis 49:24 and, "Yhwh–Tsidkenu" (the Lord Our Righteousness) in Jeremiah 33.16. Each name revealed a different aspect of his multifaceted character. The depth of meaning in each name is a rewarding study in itself, and if you undertake it, your comprehension of the nature of God will be enhanced. This is one of the wonderful things about eternity—studying the nature of our God. Learning more and more about the Lord is like studying facets of a diamond—always another angle and always more sparkling light.

The Trinity

Something that is difficult, if not impossible, for our finite minds to fully understand is the revelation of the Lord as a triunity; that is, three persons in one God. A second-century Christian scholar, Tertullian, called this revelation of God "the Trinity." The Trinity is *not* three gods—that would certainly be idolatry—but three distinct personalities making up the Godhead. The Trinity is not a concept created by Christians to deify Jesus of Nazareth but a progressive revelation. Here are some examples from the Old Testament.

1. God is shown as a plurality in creation. God said, "Let us make man in our image" (Gen. 1:26). The name for God is "Elohim," which is a plural word.
2. Probably the most quoted verse of observant Jews is Deuteronomy 6:4. It is called the schema. "Hear, O Israel: The LORD our God is one LORD." The phonetic transliteration (what the Hebrew sounds like in English) of this verse is *Sh'ma Yis-ra-el, A-do-nai E-lo-he-nu, A-do-nai echad.* The word "echad," translated as "one," is the same word used by Adam in Genesis 2:24 to reference "one flesh" as the condition of a man and wife. They are two distinct people but become "one flesh." They are one in unity not one in number.

3. The Old Testament references the "Son" specifically in several verses. For example:

> I will declare the decree: the LORD hath said unto me, Thou art my Son; this day have I begotten thee. Ask of me, and I shall give thee the heathen for thine inheritance, and the uttermost parts of the earth for thy possession. Thou shalt break them with a rod of iron; thou shalt dash them in pieces like a potter's vessel. Be wise now therefore, O ye kings: be instructed, ye judges of the earth. Serve the LORD with fear, and rejoice with trembling. Kiss the Son, lest he be angry, and ye perish from the way, when his wrath is kindled but a little. Blessed are all they that put their trust in him. (Ps. 2:7–12)

> I saw in the night visions, and, behold, one like the Son of man came with the clouds of heaven, and came to the Ancient of days, and they brought him near before him. And there was given him dominion, and glory, and a kingdom, that all people, nations, and languages, should serve him: his dominion is an everlasting dominion, which shall not pass away, and his kingdom that which shall not be destroyed. (Dan. 7:13–14)

The Spirit of God is not absent from the Old Testament either. Numerous verses picture Him present and accounted for. Consider the presence of the Lord in Isaiah: "Come ye near unto me, hear ye this; I have not spoken in secret from the beginning; from the time that it was, there am I: and now the Lord GOD, and his Spirit, hath sent me. Thus saith the LORD, thy Redeemer, the Holy One of Israel; I am the LORD thy God which teacheth thee to profit, which leadeth thee by the way that thou shouldest go" (Isa. 48:15–17).

In Isaiah 42:1, the Father speaks of His Spirit and His Chosen One: "Behold my servant, whom I uphold; mine elect, in whom my soul delighteth; I have put my spirit upon him: he shall bring forth judgment to the Gentiles."

Many other Scriptures testify to the existence of the Trinity, such as Isaiah 61:1, which is quoted by Jesus in His teaching at Nazareth (Luke 4:18) and links us to Jesus's fulfillment of the promises made to redeem Israel.

The evidence of the Trinity becomes clear in the ministry of Jesus. Although the Bible records the three members of the Godhead as appearing together at the same time, there are still those who maintain they are not distinct persons but only differing roles. In Mark 1:9–11, the Father speaks of the pleasure He has in His Son; the Son is present in the water undergoing baptism; and the Spirit descends in the form of a dove. There is strong scriptural evidence for the distinct personhood of the members of the Godhead. For example, in John 14:15, Jesus tells His disciples that He will ask the Father to send another Comforter, whom He calls "the Spirit of Truth." (The word Jesus chose to use, "another," means another of the same kind as Him). The Scripture that closes the book on the concept of roles versus persons is the prayer conversation Jesus had with His Father in the garden of Gethsemane, just hours before His arrest and crucifixion. Jesus prayed, "And he went a little further, and fell on his face, and prayed, saying, O my Father, if it be possible, let this cup pass from me: nevertheless not as I will, but as thou wilt" (Matt. 26:39).

This clearly shows there was a difference in the will of the Father and the will of the Son, who asked for another possible way to complete His assignment. The fact that He had to submit His will to the will of the Father demonstrates two persons, functioning as one (*echad*). If you want to study more about the doctrine of the Trinity, the Cappadocian Fathers of the fourth century wrote a great deal about it, answering challenges from heretical groups of their time. The end product of their work is called the Nicene Creed, completed in AD 381.

How Does the Trinity Function in the Salvation of Mankind?

Although each member of the Godhead has a distinct work in our salvation, none ever acts independently of the other. The work is accomplished by the Trinity functioning in perfect unity. The Father originates, chooses, and calls us; the Son reveals the Father and redeems us by means of His own death on the cross; and the Spirit witnesses to Christ, awakens our dead spirits, and gives us new life. There is no confusion or duplication in the work of the Trinity. It is not the Father's job to die on the cross, nor is it the Spirit's work to initiate the call. Although each member of the Trinity is a specialist, there is scriptural evidence of how they work together to achieve a purpose. For example, Romans 8:26 and Hebrews 7:25 show both the Son and the Spirit interceding with the Father on our behalf. They are united in their work, and they are united in purpose. Every member of the Trinity is involved whenever one member does something. Emphasis is given to that member whose particular work is in focus at any given time. This, of course, is a simplification of how the Trinity works in us.

How Do People Get Saved?

It is impossible to study how people get saved without marveling at the intense love of God, who reached out to mankind in such a dynamic way so that man could have fellowship with Him. It is the subject of the first Scripture verse you probably learned. "For God so loved the world that he gave His only begotten Son, that whosoever believeth in Him should not perish, but have everlasting life" (John 3:16).

In these few words, we see God's motive, His sacrifice; and His plan for salvation. When I was a child, I learned a catechism answer to the question, "Why do we love God?" The answer: "Because He first loved us." Wrapped up in His motive of love are the two commandments Jesus gave to us, by which we must live our lives. "And he answering said, Thou shalt love the Lord thy God with all thy heart, and with all thy soul, and with all thy strength, and with all thy mind; and thy neighbor as thyself" (Luke 10:27).

If anyone tries to tell you God had a different motive, such as He was lonely and wanted company, don't believe it. Love was the only motive strong enough for the Father to allow the awesome sacrifice of His Son. God is perfect and is in need of nothing. Never think His motive was anything but love.

Various denominations draw different conclusions from Scripture as to how people are saved. If the Father draws men unto Him, how does He choose whom to draw? Does He draw everyone at some time in his life? Is it fair not to call everyone? If someone is chosen, what if he doesn't respond to the call? Is a man able to resist God's call, or is salvation a foregone conclusion, once the Father draws him? Each denomination finds verses to support its particular position, but if we take the time to explore each question in depth, it is possible to lose sight of our goal of activating for evangelism. Additionally, I do not want to reinvent the wheel. There are many good works available that explore these questions. The purpose of this work is not to debate these issues or even to take a position but to examine the basic procedure God uses to take one who is dead in spirit because of sin and resurrect him into new life in Jesus Christ.

In the Beginning, God!

Just as in the opening verse of Genesis, the start of all activity begins with God. Did you ever wonder why two people will hear the exact same presentation of the gospel, and one will be deeply moved while the other is not remotely affected, finding the position of the hands on his watch more important than his position in relation to his Creator? I am convinced it is the preparation work done by the Spirit of God in response to the drawing of the Father. The Word tells us that "it is God which worketh in you both to will and to do of his good pleasure" (Phil. 2:13).

When the Father issues the invitation, the preparation work has already been accomplished in the heart. I was in my mid-thirties when I became aware that I was not really a Christian but only a crude imitation of what my parents' denomination defined a Christian to be. I believed everything I was taught concerning Jesus and completed all the rituals specified by the church, but intellectual belief was as far as it went. Though I completed all the things required by the church, I was not satisfied. Somewhere deep inside, I knew something was drastically wrong with me.

Frankly, the stories of Jesus learned in childhood haunted me. I wanted Him to mean more to me than He did. I tried every activity I could think of to make the crucifixion and resurrection deeply meaningful to me, including prolonged fasting, but somehow, despite all my efforts, I was still empty inside. I was frustrated that all my efforts were not alleviating my spiritual emptiness. In my misery, I had no idea it was a loving Father drawing me. I only knew my inner hunger was not satisfied, not by anything I did or by increasing my head knowledge. Okay, I really, really wanted what I was missing; so what was next?

Coming to the End of Myself

After close examination of my lifestyle, I reasoned that drastic changes had to be made if I was to please the Lord. I was very determined that I was now going to follow the Lord no matter what. Before you start cheering, "Praise the Lord," please understand that I hadn't the foggiest idea how I was going to do that. If you notice all the I's in my declaration, it is easy to see that failure was a given. Although my plan included the cessation of all activities I knew were not pleasing to God, I found I was powerless to achieve that goal. No matter how I tried, I could not stop doing things I knew displeased Him. I had to stop sinning if I wanted Him to love me, didn't I? Why couldn't I do what my strong-willed mind determined I should do? Like a creature caught in quicksand, the harder I tried, the deeper I sank.

After a while, I became so frustrated with failure after failure, I gave up trying and plunged into living a very hedonistic lifestyle, even worse than before. Separation from God and the punishment of hell lay before me, and there just didn't seem to be anything I could do about it. I was a prime example of John 6:44a. "No man can come to me, except the Father which hath sent me draw him."

The Work of Salvation

I will never know why—I surely did not deserve it—but God had great compassion on me. Thanks to a praying grandmother, while I was yet a horrible sinner the love and the mercy of the Father was extended to me. The drawing of the Father, coupled with the gift of repentance, brought me face-to-face with the work of Jesus on the cross. I was always a fix-it person, believing I could correct whatever was wrong by sheer willpower. On that day I was brought to the end of myself and knew that only Jesus could save me from the quagmire. I had no power over sin until Jesus became the center of my life—my only savior. It was the Father who drew me, the Son who saved me, and the Spirit who granted me the gift of eternal life. I am eternally grateful for the free gift of salvation.

Christians need to recognize a hard truth: not everyone will be saved. While it is scripturally true that God doesn't want anyone to perish, God does not always get what He wants.

"The Lord is not slack concerning his promise, as some men count slackness; but is longsuffering to us-ward, not willing that any should perish, but that all should come to repentance"(2 Peter 3:9).

"For this is good and acceptable in the sight of God our Savior; Who will have all men to be saved, and to come unto the knowledge of the truth" (1 Tim. 2:3–4).

There are people whose hearts are just so hard, they will not be saved. The Word tells us that God has mercy on those He desires (He knows the heart) and hardens others (Rom. 9:18). Be careful not to judge God. God is not arbitrary, and He is not only a God of mercy but also a God of justice. In the American legal system, we have something called mandatory sentencing. The judge may want to set someone free, but the law prescribes a sentence that must be exacted. God must pronounce a just sentence on those who have refused the only way to be pardoned; that is, trusting in the complete work of Jesus Christ.

Rejoice, and Again I Say Rejoice (Phil. 4:4)

Here are some scriptural facts that will make your heart glad: You have been given to Jesus Christ as a gift from the Father. "All that the Father giveth me shall come to me; and him that cometh to me I will in no wise cast out" (John 6:37).

You were chosen by the Father before He created the world. "According as he hath chosen us in him before the foundation of the world, that we should be holy and without blame before him in love" (Eph. 1:4).

Who Is the Father Drawing?

Activating your heart for the lost starts with becoming aware of those around you, those in your personal sphere of influence. You may have been praying "scatter-gun" prayers for your neighbors and relatives, but like any marksman, taking focus will greatly increase the chances for success. When you pray, ask the Lord for revelation knowledge of whom to target in your prayers for salvation. There is great power in agreement, especially when your prayers line up with what the Father is doing. Watch for subtle evidence of drawing. Is there an indication that God is working in someone's life? That is the person you want to target in your prayer; let that one become your daily prayer focus.

The Work of the Son in Salvation

There was a problem in the garden of God. His premier creation, man and woman, separated themselves from the holiness of God and aligned themselves with the "rebel in chief," wearing his snake-skin suit. The woman wasn't exactly sure what the Lord said about the fruit on the Tree of Knowledge of Good and Evil, so she added a prohibition to the "don't eat it" rule, just to be sure. According to the woman, the sentence of death extended to touching the fruit as well as eating it. When the serpent approached her and promised that she would become as God, knowing good and evil, she tested it out. The fruit looked good and smelled like food, and so she touched it. Since nothing happened when she broke her own addition to God's rule, she accepted this as evidence that the serpent was right. The woman ate, the man ate, and they were both now in rebellion against their Creator. Rebellion against God is a three-letter word: s-i-n! This is a familiar story and as we are well aware, judgment followed.

Something additional that followed was the promise of a Redeemer who would make things right again. This is called the "protoevangelium" (the first gospel) and is found in Genesis 3:15. Making things right again was no small accomplishment. There were legalities involved that required extraordinary action on God's part. God is perfect; man had become sinful, and a sinful man could not be in the presence of a holy

God and live. In order for that fellowship to be restored, an appropriate price needed to be paid. God had already pronounced a death sentence as the just punishment for sin. The only way fellowship with the Father could be restored was through the blood sacrifice of a sinless substitute. Over the centuries, God gave mankind the Law to show him what sin really was and how perfectly the Law had to be kept in order to enter His presence. In short, it could not be done; it was impossible because we are all born in the image of Adam, our sinful first father. It was inevitable that each one of us would fall into sin before we even knew what sin was. Still, the price for sin had to be paid by a man but not a man born with the sinful nature of Adam. This is a very basic description of the problem.

God's Solution to the Problem

"And the Word was made flesh, and dwelt among us, [and we beheld his glory, the glory as of the only begotten of the Father], full of grace and truth" (John 1:14).

"For God so loved the world, that he gave his only begotten Son, that whosoever believeth in him should not perish, but have everlasting life" (John 3:16).

"Herein is love, not that we loved God, but that he loved us, and sent his Son to be the propitiation for our sins" (1 John 4:10).

I have often made a big mistake in talking to people about God's solution for sin by making it too complicated. I want to get deep into theology instead of keeping it simple. The beauty of the gospel message is its simplicity and its complexity. Keep your response simple, and let the Holy Spirit do His work.

The sinless sacrifice for man's sin could not be a descendant of Adam, who passed down a sinful nature to all his children. God provided for a virgin to conceive through the power of the Holy Spirit. She gave birth to a son called Jesus. He was and is the Son of the highest, born without a sin nature, yet fully man, inhabiting a body of flesh. This is called the "hypostatic union." Throughout His earthly life, His righteousness was tested and tried, but He was dedicated to the mission; to become sin for us so that we could become the righteousness of God in Him (2 Cor. 5:21).

The Father draws us, and the Son makes the way for us to be saved. Our only job is to receive the work already done for us.

"He came unto his own, and his own received him not. But as many as received him, to them gave the power to become the sons of God, even to them that believe on his name" (John 1:11–12).

"And for this cause he is the mediator of the new testament, that by means of death, for the redemption of the transgressions that were under the first testament, they which are called might receive the promise of eternal inheritance" (Heb. 9:15).

"Jesus saith unto him, I am the way, the truth, and the life: no man cometh unto the Father, but by me" (John 14:6).

Making It Personal

The Father draws us to the Son, the only way of restoring fellowship with Him. The work of the third member of the Godhead, the Holy Spirit, is to put it all together for us and make it personal. Jesus told His disciples that He would send another Comforter of the same kind to them, and His function would be to reprove of sin, exemplify righteousness, and teach about judgment (John 16:8–14). This is making it personal. When you grasp the holiness of Jesus compared with your own shortcomings, you know you need a savior. When you recognize that the path you are currently on leads to eternal hell, you know you need to make a U-turn and change direction. The Holy Spirit, working in you, enables you to see these things and to open your heart to receive the remedy for sin that has been prepared for you. He will teach you all you need to know.

"But the Comforter, which is the Holy Ghost, whom the Father will send in my name, he shall teach you all things, and bring all things to your remembrance, whatsoever I have said unto you" (John 14:26).

Once the Spirit of God is welcomed into your life, He will make your dead spirit live—and live abundantly. When this happened for me, it was like a dark room that was suddenly filled with glorious light. What happens, according to the Bible, is you become brand new.

"Therefore if any man be in Christ, he is a new creature: old things are passed away; behold, all things are become new" (2 Cor. 5:17).

How many of us have said, "Oh, if I could only start over again, knowing what I know now!" The good news is, you can, and God does all the heavy lifting.

Study/Teaching Outline—God Does All the Heavy Lifting

How People Get Saved
- What is God like? (As far as we can understand)
  - God has revealed Himself in the Bible as three persons in one God.
  - Christians call this 'the Trinity.
  - *Not* three Gods—that would be idolatry—but a triunity (three persons making up the Godhead.)
  - The word Trinity is not in the Bible, but the word describes what God is like, and there are numerous biblical examples to support the doctrine.
  - We may never understand how God can be three and yet one, but there are three distinct personalities in the Bible called "God."
  - Concept of the Trinity is revealed *progressively* in the Bible.
  - Old Testament evidence references the Trinity by showing God as a plurality. Example: God said, "Let us make man in our image" (Gen.1:26). The name for God, "Elohim," is a plural word.
    - The schema uses the word 'echad' which is a plural concept.
    - "Hear, O Israel, the Lord our God is one Lord" (Deut. 6:4). It is the same word used to describe the "one flesh" concept of marriage where two distinct people

become one flesh. There are many Old Testament uses of echad, all showing plurality.

- Psalm 2:7, 12; Proverbs 30:4; and Daniel 7:13–14 reference the Son directly, and numerous Old Testament verses reference the Spirit of God; for example, Isaiah 48:16; 42:1; 61:1).

- Evidence of Trinity becomes clear in the ministry of Jesus
  - Jesus's baptism (Mark 1:9–11). The Father speaks to Jesus the Son, and the Holy Spirit descends.
    - ✓ Note: all three members of the Trinity are present at the same time.
  - Jesus speaking in John 14:15. "I [Jesus] will ask the Father, and He will give you another Counselor ... the Spirit of truth." (The Greek word for "another" means "of the same essence, divine.")
- Paul references the work of the Trinity in Titus 3:4–8a. Each person of the Trinity has a vital part to play in our salvation. It is:
  - the love, kindness and mercy of the Father
  - the saving acts of the Son
  - the washing and generation of new life from the Spirit
- Some fundamental truths about the Trinity to think about:
  - The Trinity *is not* just a way of looking at how God works. (It is what God is.)
  - Three persons comprise one God.
  - God is and always has been three distinct persons.
  - Each person of the Trinity *is fully God*; no person of the Trinity is more God or less God than any other person.
  - Each person of the Trinity, individually, has the same attributes as are spoken of as belonging to God as a whole

The work of the Trinity in salvation.

- No person of the Trinity acts independently of the others.
- Each member of the Trinity has a distinctive primary role (or work).
  - The Father originates, chooses, and calls us.

- The Son reveals the Father and redeems us by means of His own death on the cross.
- The Spirit witnesses to Christ (John 15:26), convicts of sin, awakens our dead souls, gives us new life, and delivers us to heaven.
- There is no confusion in the Godhead; no duplication
    - It is not the Son's work to call and awaken our dead souls. It is not the Father's role to die on the cross. It is not the Spirit's role to call us or to die for us.
    - According to Romans 8:26 and Hebrews 7:25, both the Son and the Spirit intercede for us with God the Father. They are united in that work.
    - Coordinated effort: Every member of the Trinity is involved whenever one member does something.
        - Whenever one member of the Trinity is doing something, all members are involved in doing it.
        - Emphasis is given to that member whose particular work it is to do that thing.

The Process of Salvation—How Do People Get Saved?

*Note: Various denominations have different ideas on how people are chosen and the ability of man to respond. Our purpose is not to debate these issues, so we will avoid controversy and cover only very basic areas substantiated by Scripture.

- **It all begins with Father. He is the initiator.**
    - The Father must draw. "No man can come to me, except the Father which hath sent me draw him: and I will raise him up at the last day" (John 6:44).
    - Why? What is God's reason for saving us? (John 3:16)
        - The situation: Mankind's fall into sin left him separated from God.
        - Reconciliation must be made between mankind and the Father, and repentance is toward God.

- Salvation is motivated by God's love for us and came at a great cost to the Father (John 3:16).
- "God so loved the world that He gave His only begotten Son, that whoever believes in Him should not perish but have everlasting life."
- Reject any comments about what God "needed." He is perfect and in need of *nothing*. (He didn't save you because He was lonely.)

° Hard truth: Not everyone will be saved.

- God doesn't want anyone to perish (2 Peter 3:9; 1 Tim. 2:3–4), but God doesn't always get what He wants.
- There are people whose hearts are so hard, they will not be saved.

° God has mercy on those He desires, and He hardens those He desires (Rom. 9:18).

° God has provided testimony to His power and divine being that all may see (Rom. 1:20).

° Don't judge God. God is not arbitrary, and He is just. A judge may want to set a person free, but the law requires he execute judgment (mandatory sentencing).

- God can lovingly desire all to be saved, but He must also execute righteous judgment on those who have not trusted in Christ Jesus.
- God is infinite, and His ways are not ours. He has reasons for doing what He does.
- The knowledge of God's divine nature is available through nature and conscience so that man is without excuse for rejecting his Creator (Ps. 19:1–4; Rom. 1:20).
- God knows the heart. Like Pharaoh, when the heart is hardened, the Holy Spirit conviction of sin and need for salvation will not be heard.

° Jesus spoke in parables so that people would not repent and be forgiven (Mark 4:10–12).

- One way the Father draws us is by giving revelation knowledge.

° Peter's confession: "He said to them, 'But who do you say that I am?' Simon Peter answered, 'You are the Christ, the Son of the living God.' And Jesus said to him, 'Blessed are you, Simon Barjona, because flesh and blood did not reveal this to you, but My Father who is in heaven'" (Matt. 16:15–16).

○ Our prayer for those targeted: "That the God of our Lord Jesus Christ, the Father of glory, may give unto you the spirit of wisdom and revelation in the knowledge of him" (Eph. 1:17).

○ God gives understanding: "No man can come to me, except the Father that sent me draws him: and I will raise him up in the last day. It is written in the prophets, 'And they shall all be taught of God. Every one that has heard from the Father, and has learned, comes unto me'" (John 6:44– 45).

Rejoice! You are a gift to Jesus from the Father.

• "Ye have not chosen me, but I have chosen you, and ordained you, that ye should go and bring forth fruit, and that your fruit should remain: that whatsoever ye shall ask of the Father in my name, he may give it you" (John 15:16).

• "According as He hath chosen us in him before the foundation of the world, that we should be holy and without blame before him in love" (Eph.1:4).

• "All that the Father giveth me shall come to me; and him that cometh to me I will in no wise cast out" (John 6:37).

• Our job is to become more aware of those around us. Is there some indication that God is working in their lives? Focus your prayer requests for them.

The work of the Son in salvation

• Jesus is "the Way" God provided to reconcile mankind to Him. "For God so loved the world, that he gave his only begotten Son, that whosoever believeth in him should not perish, but have everlasting life" (John 3:16).

• Jesus is "the only way" God could satisfy the debt of sin and offer forgiveness. God the Son, motivated by love, came to be the sinless sacrifice for our sins (Col. 1:15; John 15:13; Rom. 3:24–26).

- God's righteous sentence for sin is death (Rom. 6:23).
- Under the Law of Moses (really, it is God's law), an innocent substitute was sacrificed to temporarily cover individual and national sin.
- Blood sacrifice of innocent substitute was required as a "type" and "shadow" of the work of the Son.

• How the Son qualifies as our innocent substitute: The Lord Jesus Christ was born of a virgin and therefore did not inherit the "sin nature" from a sinful human father. (A sin nature means sinning is inevitable. We have *all* sinned (Rom. 3:23), except for Jesus (2 Cor. 5:21).

• The incarnation means He came as God and became man. This is called the "hypostatic union" (John 1:1; 14).

- He had to be a man because death was the penalty, and God cannot die.
- He had to be God because when a human dies, he dies for his own sin, and only someone who is sinless can pay for the sins of another.
- Jesus, God's Son, was the only sinless sacrifice possible to substitute for us. There is no other (Acts 4:12).
- Jesus's purpose was to save sinners: "For God sent not his Son into the world to condemn the world; but that the world through him might be saved" (John 3:17).
  - The crucifixion didn't just "happen." It was God's plan from the foundation of the world.
  - "Who killed Jesus?" Was it the Romans? Was it the Jews? The correct answer is, the Father killed Jesus. "Yet it pleased the Lord to bruise Him, He has put Him to grief" (Isa. 53:10).
  - Jesus is the door to the Father: "I am the door: by me if any man enter in, he shall be saved, and shall go in and out, and find pasture" (John 10:9).

- There is nothing more required for salvation to satisfy the justice of God. Jesus proclaimed "It is finished" from the cross (John 19:30).
- The importance of the resurrection: the Father showed the world that Jesus's sacrifice was accepted as payment for our sins when He raised Him from the grave (1 Cor. 15:4).
  - Our sins have been paid for. The gap between God and man has been bridged.
  - Without Jesus there is no salvation and our faith in anything else is worthless (1 Cor. 15–19). He is our salvation (Luke 2:29) and the only way to the Father. "I am the way, the truth, and the life. No one cometh unto the Father, but by Me" (John 14:6).

The work of the Holy Spirit in salvation
- Jesus outlined the work of the Holy Spirit.
  "Nevertheless I tell you the truth; It is expedient for you that I go away: for if I go not away, the Comforter will not come unto you; but if I depart, I will send him unto you. And when he is come, he will reprove the world of sin, and of righteousness, and of judgment: Of sin, because they believe not on me; Of righteousness, because I go to my Father, and ye see me no more; Of judgment, because the prince of this world is judged" (John 16:7–11).
- When the Father draws, mankind must be brought to recognize his need for a Savior.
- The conviction of the Holy Spirit ("to reprove of sin, righteousness and judgment") shows man the truth about his sinful condition and eternal destiny.
- It is the Holy Spirit that regenerates man when he accepts the sacrifice of Jesus and quickens his spirit (John 6:63).

The work of man in the salvation process
- There is *nothing* you can do to save yourself. All parts of the salvation process are a gift of God. (He draws, provides the way, enables understanding, and facilitates repentance.) We call this

grace. "For by grace are ye saved through faith; and that not of yourselves: it is the gift of God: Not of works, lest any man should boast" (Eph. 2:8–9).

- Note: It is essential to treat the unsaved with love and to pray for them because they are blind to the gospel. They truly do not understand. Consider what Paul says about the Jews: "For I would not, brethren, that ye should be ignorant of this mystery, lest ye should be wise in your own conceits; that blindness in part is happened to Israel, until the fulness of the Gentiles be come in" (Rom. 11:25).
- Man's part is strictly to *respond* to the call of God and, in turn, call upon Him. "For whosoever shall call upon the name of the Lord shall be saved" (Rom. 10:13–15).
- Our part in evangelism is to make God's plan known: "How then shall they call on him in whom they have not believed? and how shall they believe in him of whom they have not heard? and how shall they hear without a preacher? And how shall they preach, except they be sent? as it is written, How beautiful are the feet of them that preach the gospel of peace, and bring glad tidings of good things!" (Rom. 10:14–15).
- The requirement for salvation is *heart* belief in the finished work of Jesus Christ and confessing that belief. "That if thou shalt confess with thy mouth the Lord Jesus, and shalt believe in thine heart that God hath raised him from the dead, thou shalt be saved. For with the heart man believeth unto righteousness; and with the mouth confession is made unto salvation" (Rom. 10:9–10).
  - Note: This kind of confession is not just repeating casual words but indicates a change of heart and direction.
  - Just "saying" a sinner's prayer is not enough. Belief must be *in the heart*.

What is the mark of a real Christian?
- Just saying you are a Christian does not mean you *are* one.
- Real Christians are:
  - led by the Spirit. "For as many as are led by the Spirit of God, they are the sons of God" (Rom. 8:14).

- ◦ If you are led by the Spirit, you are His.
- Real Christians have the Holy Spirit within.
  - ◦ "But ye are not in the flesh, but in the Spirit, if so be that the Spirit of God dwell in you. Now if any man have not the Spirit of Christ, he is none of His"(Rom. 8:9).
  - ◦ You become a child of God when the Spirit indwells you.

How did people get saved before Jesus?
- Before Jesus accomplished the work of salvation, Old Testament saints looked forward to the Messiah in *faith*. They believed the promises of God to send a Redeemer.
  - ◦ The very first promise was given in the garden of Eden (Gen. 3:15). It is called the "protoevangelium."
  - ◦ Old Testament saints were saved by faith in the promises of God.
  - ◦ New Testament saints are saved by faith in the fulfillment of that promise.
- No one is saved by keeping the Law.
  - ◦ A common misconception is that Jews were saved by keeping the Law. But Scripture says this is not true. "Now it is evident that no one is justified before God by the law, for 'The righteous shall live by faith'" (Gal. 3:11).
  - ◦ This passage applies to both the Old and New Testament.
    - Paul quotes Habakkuk 2:4 that the just shall live by faith. Salvation by faith, apart from the Law, was an Old Testament principle too.
    - Paul taught that the purpose of the Law was to serve as a "tutor to bring us to Christ, that we might be justified by faith" (Gal. 3:24).
  - ◦ In Romans 3:20, Paul states, "Therefore by the deeds of the law there shall no flesh be justified in his sight: for by the law is the knowledge of sin."
  - ◦ The Law was never given to save anyone; but only to make us aware of sin.

- The Ten Commandments show us we cannot keep the Ten Commandments.
  - People in the Old Testament were saved by faith, just like people today (Isa. 55:7).
  - Abraham was not saved by works, but Abraham believed God, and it was credited to him as righteousness (Gen. 15:6; Rom. 4:3).
  - Abraham lived over four hundred years before the Law was given.
  - David was also saved by faith (Rom. 4:6–8, quotes Ps. 32:1–2).
  - Paul ties Old Testament faith to New Testament faith (Rom. 4:23–24).

Summary: There is only one gospel message and one way to salvation. Throughout history people have tried to pervert the gospel by adding human works to it, requiring certain things to be done to "earn" salvation. But the Bible's clear message is that *the way of salvation has always been through faith.* In the Old Testament, it was faith in the promise that God would someday send a Savior. Those who lived in Old Testament times looked forward to the Messiah and believed God's promise of the coming servant of the Lord (Isa. 53). Those who exercised such faith were saved. Today, we look back on the life, death, and resurrection of the Savior and are saved by faith in His completed work of atonement for our sins (Rom. 10:9–10). Then, as now, God did *all* the heavy lifting.

CHAPTER FOUR

The Dirty Word

When Jesus took up residence in my heart, He gave me a new life and changed my entire outlook. Joy replaced the empty feelings that kept me in bondage for so many years. Since I had been a pew dweller in a church since early childhood, the term "born again" was not completely unfamiliar, but I had no idea what it really meant. I can't remember hearing any teaching on the matter; it was just a phrase occasionally mentioned when a certain Scripture was read during the ritual. Actually, I was angry at the church for being so critical about external matters but never teaching me about the necessity for a personal relationship with Jesus Christ. After experiencing the new birth, I planned on interrogating the pastor of my parents' church as to why he never taught about the subject of regeneration. It took about two weeks to realize that the church did not teach about the new birth because they did not know about the new birth. All the necessary doctrine was present in ritual, documents, and history, but it had no practical meaning to the leadership. My anger changed to sadness and compassion for those who were trapped in religion, yet missed the entire point. I knew I could no longer stay in the church denomination supported by my parents.

Where Should I Go, Lord?

Finding a dynamic born-again church was no easy task. I was invited to attend a nondenominational fellowship in Brooklyn, New York, with the caveat that it was very different from my past experience, and I might find it a little bit of a shock. That was an understatement. The celebratory worship in this church was untamed and unstructured. People not only clapped their hands to the worship songs but got up and danced. Spontaneous shouts of "Praise God," "Hallelujah," and "Glory to Jesus" punctuated the music. I thought these people were absolutely out of their minds, yet the presence of the Lord in the worship was unmistakable. The focus was clearly on Jesus, and that is what made it palatable to someone whose church experience more or less frowned on any display of joy in the congregation. Truthfully, I was shocked, but as long as Jesus was honored, I was not offended. It was a wonderful experience but regretfully, it was not feasible to be part of this congregation because of the distance from my home.

As a new believer, I needed to be discipled. For about two years before actually being born again, my focus was on study of the Bible. In past years, I'd read the Bible but did not understand what it was all about. The words were clear enough, but for some reason I could not grasp the meaning. Unlike previous readings of the Scriptures, this time the Bible came alive with supernatural illumination. I came to understand 1 Corinthians 2:14. "But the natural man receiveth not the things of the Spirit of God: for they are foolishness unto him: neither can he know them, because they are spiritually discerned." God was giving me a degree of spiritual discernment, and His Word was becoming real to me. This time of my life was special. The Lord provided not only grounding in His Word but fellowship with other believers as well. I don't remember how I first became aware of a group of believers meeting for devotions at break time on the job, but somehow I found myself attending a daily gathering. Two other new believers, who would have a dynamic impact in my life, were part of this impromptu fellowship. Andrea was, on the surface, opposite to me in many areas, yet we were so much the same that we began calling each other not only sister but twin sister. Our friendship has endured more than thirty years, and although she has returned to her native country of Trinidad, we have remained close through the wonders of electronics. The second new believer was Leo, a young man so totally given over to the Lord that he motivated Andrea and me to greater study and ultimately into evangelistic outreach. All three of us were management employees of the same major utility company, working in different capacities.

One morning after devotions, Andrea succinctly stated a problem we were both experiencing. She said, "You know, my prayer life stinks!" I had to confess, so did mine. Andrea and I resolved that we would no longer have lunch but that we would find a place to meet for prayer during the hour allotted. Before long, others joined us, and the Lord moved in impressive ways. Reports of miracle healings increased the number of believers at our lunchtime prayer meetings. People came from other companies in our building and from other locations in Midtown Manhattan. Ministries were birthed from that little prayer meeting. One man, delivered from homosexuality, opened a Christian bookstore, and a woman originally from Panama began a hospital evangelistic ministry, with several miracle healings happening after she laid hands on the sick. Soon, the presence of our little prayer group became obvious to higher management—too obvious to survive. The numbers attending caused us to move from office to office and finally to a conference room. It wasn't long before we were locked out of all facilities, even a little-used stairwell. Our prayer meeting was unequivocally shut down.

Enter Leo into the mix. Leo's heart was always in street ministry, and he took this occasion to voice his opinion that the Lord had allowed the prayer meeting to be shut down because He wanted us to go out on the streets to minister during the lunch hour. I was appalled. Go out on the streets and talk to strangers? Not me! I did not want to go. Study and prayer were what I wanted to do. Evangelism was a dirty word as far as I was concerned.

A Common Condition

If you want to guarantee poor attendance at an event, connect it to active evangelism. I was not alone in not wanting to reach out to unbelievers. Like so many others, I was willing to contribute finances so that someone else would do the job, but actually doing it was quite another thing. When we think of evangelism, the first thought that comes to us is usually the foreign mission field, but the fact is, the mission field is on our own doorstep. We don't have to think hard to find reasons why we cannot go on the foreign mission field; after all, by definition it's "foreign." However, the street where you live is not foreign and is still part of this world.

Why are we so resistant to being obedient to the command of the Lord? Grasping the misery of a life without Jesus and the eternal destiny of the lost should be sufficient motivation to overcome any resistance on our part. Why isn't it? Understanding that the burden of salvation is not on our shoulders but that the Lord does the heavy work should relieve us of a fear of failure, so why is it we don't want to become "fishers of men."

Fear of Fishing

The word "evangelist" frequently gives rise to negative images of big-haired television preachers asking you to send them money, eccentric street preachers shouting about hellfire and damnation, and door-to-door cultic missionaries interrupting a peaceful Saturday morning. Most of us take a look at these methods and decide we cannot relate because that's just not us. While certain methods may be repugnant to you, they may be just the approach needed to convey the words a certain person needs to hear. Evangelism takes many forms because there are many different kinds of people, and the Lord loves them all. Different fish require different methods of fishing. Never assume that everyone is the same as you and will respond in the same way you do. If you question the technique, ask the correct question: is the gospel being preached?

I once heard the testimony of a Jewish man, Jerry Kaufman, who was a notorious drunk. Jerry found himself so drunk that he slept curbside on the Grand Concourse, a major thoroughfare in the Bronx. One day he awoke from his alcoholic stupor, and he picked up a gospel tract that had been discarded near his unconscious body. He sat on the curb and read the words discarded by another but meant for him. He was gloriously saved and over the course of his life became the pastor of a fellowship that met in a former synagogue on the Grand Concourse, not far from where he'd slept on the curb. When Jerry Kaufman left this planet, many could point to him as the messenger the Lord used to bring them to salvation. Tracing back only one step, many came to know the Lord because someone cared enough to spend time giving out gospel tracts in the Bronx. The Word of the Lord never comes back void but always accomplishes God's purpose (Isa. 55:11).

Whatever your personality, there is always something you can do to promote the kingdom of God. Evangelism isn't scary; it is simply sharing your faith, and there are people in your sphere of influence that you can reach. If we can grasp the simplicity of sharing faith, the fear level becomes drastically reduced. Can you tell your friend about what the Lord has done for you? Your life belongs to the Lord, which means everything you say and do needs to be submitted to Him. Your life must become an open Bible to those you meet. That is pretty frightening because we are all projects under construction, saying and doing things that do not glorify the Lord. But even your renovation process can be a testimony to the grace of the Lord. Don't be afraid to go fishing. In your prayer time, ask the Lord to give you opportunity to share your faith.

Evangelism: Notches on the Handle of Your Gospel Gun

When I was a child, western movies flooded the few available television channels. There were many behavioral conventions that helped the viewer navigate the stories. The good guy wore a white hat and sported fancy silver-handled guns. The bad guy wore a black hat and cut notches in the handle of his six-shooter for every man he shot. Well-meaning believers and some ministers can be just like the bad guy, cutting a notch for every person led to say a prayer asking for salvation. Numbers become the criterion for success, and when numbers are what count, we will do anything to get them. We deceive others when we assure them that reciting a prayer makes them "saved" when, in fact, there is no real repentance, no true faith, and no change of life. We encourage the individual to have faith in the act of saying a prayer instead of the finished work of Jesus. A follow-up of those who claim to have made a decision for Christ sadly reveals that a high percentage does not follow Jesus after a short time. This kind of "evangelism by numbers" is man-centered and strays from being focused on the Lord Jesus Christ. We make Jesus nothing more than a ticket to ride the train to heaven or a fire-insurance policy. We are called to make disciples, not to get people to say a guided prayer. When someone says a sinner's prayer, our job has only begun. Stop looking at the numbers. God is not in the "body count" business but is in the business of making sons (Rom. 8:14).

Addressing the Fear Factor

J. Warner Wallace is a retired Los Angeles cold-case detective. He was a confirmed atheist until he decided to apply the same techniques he used as a cold-case detective to the case of the resurrection of Jesus Christ. His intention was to prove the Bible account to be erroneous and therefore show Christianity was based on falsehood. His investigation proved exactly the opposite, and Mr. Wallace became a staunch believer. The Lord uses him in the area of teaching apologetics, a ten-dollar word that simply means making a case for what you believe. This is something we are all called to do (1 Peter 3:15).

Mr. Wallace now teaches apologetics to teenagers at a summer camp, preparing young men and women to share their faith. The top reasons teenagers give for not wanting to evangelize are very similar to the list given by adults in a corresponding survey. The reasons given all reflect the same concern: how will I appear to the outside world?

1. "I'm afraid I will look or sound stupid."
2. "I'm afraid I will forget what to say, or I will say the wrong thing."
3. "I'm afraid I will get cussed out by someone I meet."

4. "I'm afraid I will not know how to start the conversation, and it will be awkward."
5. "I'm afraid someone will want to fight me."

Most fears expressed by adults are emotionally centered in our own desire to be comfortable. Adults expressed:

1. fear of rejection;
2. fear of offending and losing a friendship;
3. feeling inadequate—not having the right answers;
4. perceptions—fear of what others will think of them;
5. being considered arrogant because they say that Jesus is the only way; and
6. vulnerability—having their own shortcomings, weaknesses, and hypocrisy scrutinized.

Settling the Issues

Whatever fear you experience, the remedy is the same and can be found in the motive for sharing your faith. "There is no fear in love; but perfect love casteth out fear: because fear hath torment. He that feareth is not made perfect in love" (1 John 4:18).

To overcome fear, check out your love quotient. Our purpose must be perfect love. If a mother sees her child in imminent danger from an oncoming truck, she will not consider her own safety but will do all in her power to rescue her child. When we consider that the lost are in danger, exercising the love of Jesus means overcoming any reticence on our part.

As for embarrassment, consider what people thought of Jesus on the road to Calvary. "Surely he hath borne our griefs, and carried our sorrows: yet we did esteem him stricken, smitten of God, and afflicted" (Isa. 53:4).

Check out your willingness meter. Jesus was rejected, mocked, ridiculed, stripped, beaten, and ultimately executed. Chances are you will not have to undergo the extremes that Jesus did, but we are His servants and must be willing to be like our Master (Matt. 10:25). Whose opinion really counts? "Whosoever therefore shall confess me before men, him will I confess also before my Father which is in heaven. But whosoever shall deny me before men, him will I also deny before my Father which is in heaven" (Matt. 10:32–33).

"What if they reject me?" you may ask. There is no "what if" about this question. You will be rejected. Consider that Jesus was rejected too. Religious leaders rejected Him (Mark 8:31), His friends and family rejected Him (Mark 6:4), and even the greater part of the whole world rejects Him (Matt. 24:9). When you are rejected, realize that the target is not you but Jesus. This is what our Lord said to his disciples when He sent them out to minister: "He that heareth you heareth me; and he that despiseth you despiseth me; and he that despiseth me despiseth him that sent me" (Luke 10:16).

Here I Am, Lord

It is important to settle it in your spirit ahead of time that no matter what fears the Enemy brings to mind, you will be obedient to the Lord's command. Admit your fears, because you can't hide anything from the Lord anyway. A Hebrew word covers the necessary attitude for a starting point. *Hineni* (pronounced he-*nay*-nee) is simply translated, "Here I am." But some rabbis, especially in messianic congregations, teach the word has a much deeper meaning. Hineni means "I am here for you fully with trust and vulnerability to do whatever you ask of me." Abraham answered, "Hineni," when the Lord called him to sacrifice his son Isaac (Gen. 22:11). When the Lord called Jacob, he responded, "Hineni" (Gen. 31:11; 46:2). Moses heard his name called out from a burning bush and answered, "Hineni" (Ex. 3:4), and Isaiah responded to the vision of the Lord with "hineni"—here I am, Lord; send me (Isa. 6).

The true starting point to sharing your faith is a willingness to obey. Will you answer "hineni"—Lord, I am here for you fully with trust and vulnerability to do whatever you ask of me?

Study/Teaching Outline Chapter Four—Dirty Word

Why Is "Evangelism" a Dirty Word?

- Church members respond in numbers for outings and activities but few report for active evangelism. Yet Jesus called His followers to be "fishers of men" (Matt. 4:18–19; Mark 1:14–20).
- Why are we reluctant to go fishing?
- The word "evangelism" conjures up images of things we don't like.
  - Big-haired TV preachers asking you to send them money
  - Loud and sweaty street preachers talking about hellfire and damnation
  - Door-to-door cult missionaries interrupting life with false teaching
- Evangelism takes many forms, and there are many different kinds of people.
- Different kinds of fish require different methods (different kinds of bait).
  - While a certain method may be repugnant to you, it may be exactly the method needed for others to hear.
  - "Different strokes for different folks."
  - Don't assume that everyone is the same as you and will respond the same way.
- Changing the word picture in your mind.
- Understand that evangelism is simply sharing your faith.
- Your uniqueness means there are those with whom you will be able to share your faith that others cannot easily reach.
- Lifestyle evangelism: being an "open Bible" to those in your sphere of influence.
  - You don't have to go to Africa to be a missionary. Your mission field is on your doorstep.
- Evangelism can be either man-centered or God-centered.
  - Man-centered evangelism bases its success on number of decisions.

- ◦ When numbers are the criterion, we will do whatever it takes to get numbers.
- The problem with numbers:
  - ◦ Many people have made their decisions for Christ and said the "sinner's prayer," but there is no repentance involved.
  - ◦ There is no change of life—no true repentance, no true faith.
  - ◦ We think the job is done and declare them to be saved.
  - ◦ We deceive them because we encourage them to have faith in the act of saying a certain prayer at a certain time instead of true faith in the finished work of the cross.
  - ◦ Jesus becomes nothing more than a ticket to board the train for heaven or a fire-insurance policy.
- We are commanded to "make disciples," not to get numbers.
  - ◦ God's not in the "body count" business but in making sons (receptacles for the indwelling of His Holy Spirit).
  - ◦ "Go ye therefore, and teach all nations, baptizing them in the name of the Father, and of the Son, and of the Holy Ghost: Teaching them to observe all things whatsoever I have commanded you: and, lo, I am with you always, even unto the end of the world. Amen" (Matt. 28:19–20).
  - ◦ Remember the biblical definition of a Christian. "For as many as are led by the Spirit of God, they are the sons of God" (Rom. 8:14).
- Our job is not done when they have said a prayer; it has only begun.

Fear—the Common Factor.
  - ◦ Fear is common to all age groups.
  - ◦ J. Warner Wallace is a retired L. A. cold-case homicide detective who was a confirmed atheist until his salvation.
    - ◦ He examined the life of Jesus, applying the same skills a detective uses.
    - ◦ The spiritual "cold case" that led to his conversion is the resurrection of Jesus Christ.

- Since his conversion and entrance into the ministry, he has taught all age groups how to make a case for their faith.
  ◦ Apologetics—an expensive word describing a scriptural task.
    ◦ Apologetics: the discipline of defending a position (often religious) through the systematic use of information.
    ◦ Biblical mandate: "But sanctify the Lord God in your hearts: and be ready always to give an answer to every man that asketh you a reason of the hope that is in you with meekness and fear" (1 Peter 3:15).
  ◦ J. Warner Wallace teaches evangelism and apologetics to teenagers at a summer camp. The following are the reasons given by the teens for not wanting to evangelize.
    ◦ "I'm afraid I will look or sound stupid."
    ◦ "I'm afraid I will forget what to say, or I will say the wrong thing."
    ◦ "I'm afraid I will get cussed out by someone I meet."
    ◦ "I'm afraid I won't know how to start the conversation, and it will be awkward."
    ◦ "I'm afraid someone will want to fight me!"
  ◦ Wallace observed that:
    ▪ Students expressed some of the same fears as their older counterparts.
    ▪ Both young and mature Christians expressed fears centered in their concern for how they were going to appear to the world around them.
    ▪ Most fears are centered in our emotions.
  ◦ Common fears expressed by adults and teenagers.
    ▪ Fear of rejection
    ▪ Fear of offending and losing a friendship
    ▪ Feeling inadequate (not having the needed answers)
    ▪ Perceptions—fear of what others will think about them
    ▪ Being seen as arrogant because they say Jesus is the only way
    ▪ Vulnerability—their own weaknesses, hypocrisies, inadequacies, and personal doubts.

- ○ Most of our fear of evangelism is centered on our own desire to be comfortable, and nothing is more uncomfortable than being embarrassed.

Starting point: hineni
- • Admit your fears. You can't hide anything from the Lord.
- • Present yourself before the Lord.
  - ○ Present yourself: "hineni"—Hebrew word, pronounced he-*nay*-nee
  - ○ Translated as "here I am." In original language.
  - ○ Some messianic rabbis teach it had a much deeper meaning.
    - • Hineni means, "I am here for you fully with trust and vulnerability to do whatever you ask of me."
  - ○ Abraham answered "hineni" when God called him to sacrifice Isaac (Gen. 22:11).
  - ○ Jacob responded to the Lord's call (Gen. 31:11; 46:2).
  - ○ Moses responded to God, who called out of the burning bush (Ex. 3:4).
  - ○ Isaiah's vision of the Lord responded, "Hineni"—"Here I am; send me" (Isa. 6).
- • Starting point to overcome fear is your willingness to obey.
- • The Lord's command is for us to make disciples. Will you answer "Hineni"? "I am here for you fully with trust and vulnerability to do whatever you ask of me."

Settling some issues within ourselves first!
- • Our motive must be perfect love. Perfect love casts out fear. "There is no fear in love; but perfect love casteth out fear: because fear hath torment. He that feareth is not made perfect in love" (1 John 4:18).
  - ○ Example of love motive: A mother, seeing her child in imminent danger of being run over, will not consider her own safety but will run into the street to save him from harm.
- • If we are motivated by the perfect love of Jesus, our fears will be driven out!

- Remember the eternal destiny of the lost. They are in as much danger as the little child in the street.
- What about our embarrassment?
  ○ What did the people think of Jesus on the road to Calvary? "Surely he hath borne our griefs, and carried our sorrows: yet we did esteem him stricken, smitten of God, and afflicted" (Isa. 53:4).
  ○ Whose opinion really counts?
    "Whosoever therefore shall confess me before men, him will I confess also before my Father which is in heaven. But whosoever shall deny me before men, him will I also deny before my Father which is in heaven" (Matt. 10:32–33).
- Check your willingness meter.
- Jesus was rejected, mocked, ridiculed, and ultimately executed.
  ○ Chances are, we will not have to suffer any of these things to any degree, but as servants we must be willing to be like the Master.
    "It is enough for the disciple that he be as his master, and the servant as his lord. If they have called the master of the house Beelzebub, how much more shall they call them of his household?"(Matt. 10:25).
- Take up your cross to follow Him. He empowers you when you are willing. "And he said to them all, If any man will come after me, let him deny himself, and take up his cross daily, and follow me" (Luke 9:23).

Rejection: what if they reject me?
- Counting the cost: Yes you will have to deal with rejection.
  ○ Religious leaders rejected Jesus."And he began to teach them, that the Son of man must suffer many things, and be rejected of the elders, and of the chief priests, and scribes, and be killed, and after three days rise again" (Mark 8:31).
  ○ Rejection by family and friends. "A prophet is not without honor, but in his own country, and among his own kin, and in his own house" (Mark 6:4).

- ○ Hated by the world. "A disciple is not above his master; but everyone, after he has been made perfect, will be like his master" (Luke 6:40). "And ye shall be hated of all nations for my name's sake" (Matt. 24:9).
- Realize it is *not you* being rejected but Jesus.

  "He that heareth you heareth me; and he that despiseth you despiseth me; and he that despiseth me despiseth him that sent me" (Luke 10:16).
  - ○ Settle it in your spirit. If I am embarrassed, so was Jesus.
  - ○ If I am rejected, it is Jesus they reject, not me!
  - ○ These things may happen, but you will have been obedient to the command.
  - ○ Hineni—"Here I am, Lord! I am here for you fully, with trust and vulnerability to do whatever you ask of me."

CHAPTER FIVE

Yes, You Can!

During that honeymoon period, when my relationship with the Lord was brand new, I enjoyed spending my evenings sprawled out on the living room carpet for hours at a time, just praying and worshipping. I lived alone, but with Jesus in my life, I no longer felt alone. It was truly a blessed time for me. Evenings became an intimate time with the Lord, and I experienced rewarding human fellowship with friends at work. I felt useful in the kingdom of God as our lunchtime prayer meeting grew, both in numbers and spiritual power.

Because things were going so well, change was not only unwelcome but threatening. Unfortunately, the dreaded alterations came about abruptly. We no longer were able to find a room to accommodate the prayer group, and so the lunchtime meetings were suspended. To add intensity to my feelings of disenfranchisement, Leo proclaimed that this change "had to be God's will" because He obviously wanted us out on the streets, doing evangelism. His conclusion was certainly not obvious to me. Since I was a "newbie" in the faith, I did not have a deep familiarity with how God worked, but it did not seem to be a good thing for a dynamic prayer meeting, yielding supernatural results, to be canceled. Leo may have been eager to hit the streets, but when it came to my going out, all I could think of was the lyrics of a song I once heard: "Please Mr. Custer, I don't wanna go!"

I was raised in New York City in a section of the Bronx that was less than fashionable and less than safe. My parents were diligent about protecting me, and like others of my generation, I soon learned fear-based survival techniques. Paramount among these was the charge, "Don't talk to strangers!" In fact, once I strayed more than a city block from home, I learned never to make eye contact with anyone I did not know. If a stranger should have the audacity to speak to me, I would ignore him and keep walking on my way, perhaps a little faster than before. These instructions were impressed upon me all of my young life; clearly, they did not provide a very good foundation for street evangelism. Before I could function effectively, a great deal of deep-seated fear had to be overcome, and at age thirty-five, I didn't know if it could ever be conquered. I decided to dismiss Leo's idea as "fine for him but not for me."

One evening, during my time of at-home worship, I listened to some of the music of Keith Green. He wrote a song titled "Asleep in the Light," and it seemed the lyrics were directed specifically to me. They hit home with the thrust of a brakeless eighteen-wheeler.

Keith Green—Asleep in the Light

Do you see, do you see all the people sinking down?
Don't you care, don't you care, are you gonna let them drown?
How can you be so numb not to care if they come?
You close your eyes and pretend the job's done

Bless me Lord, bless me Lord, You know it's all I ever hear
No one aches, no one hurts, no one even sheds one tear
But He cries, He weeps, He bleeds, and He cares for your needs
And you just lay back and keep soaking it in

Oh, can't you see it's such a sin? 'Cause He brings people to your door
And you turn them away as you smile and say
God bless you, be at peace, and all heaven just weeps
'Cause Jesus came to your door you've left Him out in the street

Open up, open up, and give yourself away
You see the need, you hear the cries so how can you delay?
God's calling and you're the one, but like Jonah you run
He's told you to speak but you keep holding it in

Can't you see it's such a sin?
The world is sleeping in the dark that the church just can't fight
'Cause it's asleep in the light
How can you be so dead, when you've been so well fed
Jesus rose from the grave and you, you can't even get out of bed
Jesus rose from the dead, come on, get out of your bed

How can you be so numb not to care if they come
You close your eyes and pretend the job's done
You close your eyes and pretend the job's done
Don't close your eyes, don't pretend the job's done[2]

I had to confront my own sin. Fear and lack of love made me a fat-cat Christian, soaking up all the good stuff and refusing to be obedient to His charge. Like Jonah, I was making excuses and running in the opposite direction. I wanted to bed down in a safe ministerial position in the pulpit of a church. As a traditional minister, I would not have to confront strangers outside of a controlled environment. I could just keep on soaking in all the benefits of a relationship with the Lord, without much risk. Truly, Jesus rose from the dead, and I didn't want to get out of bed.

---

[2] Green, Keith. "Asleep in the Light" Song ID 364, Copywrite@1979 Birdwing Music (ASCAP) Ears to Hear Music (ASCAP) Universal Music-Brentwood Benson Publ. (ASCAP) (adm. at CapitolCMGPublishing.com) all rights reserved. Used by permission

Getting Prepared

Once resolved that obedience to His call trumped my fears, I decided to learn all I could about street evangelism before venturing out into the wilds of Midtown Manhattan. I learned of a seminar to be held in Rome, New York, conducted by a man who wrote the book known as the Bible of street evangelism. I read Jonathan Gainsbrugh's book *Take Him to the Streets* and signed up for the intensive training course. The book was directed at younger people, many of whom were enmeshed in drug problems. I was somewhat overwhelmed by this and looked for a possible excuse to weasel out of participating. While it was true I had earned a postgraduate degree in sin in my own past, none of it involved street drugs. I wondered how useful I would be if I could not relate to such a foreign culture. Seemed like a good excuse to bail out, but then I realized that many missionaries also wonder if they will be able to relate to foreign cultures. I would just have to learn and depend on God to equip me for the task.

The content of the course was useful. Friday night and Saturday morning were devoted to lecture and study, and Saturday afternoon was set aside for a trip into town for actual street witnessing. When Saturday morning's teaching concluded, Jonathan announced that the van would be leaving for town in less than twenty minutes. More important, he said that participation in the street outing was purely voluntary. This was music to my ears, for I did not feel properly prepared to "take Him to the streets"—at least not yet. My plan for the afternoon was to return to the dorm to study all the material that had been distributed during class time. Yes, that would be a better choice, I thought. I gathered all the paperwork together and stopped off at the comfort station before returning to the room. As I entered the privacy of the restroom, I heard a very stern voice, loud and distinct. "You get downstairs *now*, and get on that van before it leaves!" Whoa! The voice was clear—could it have been audible, or was it in my spirit? I looked around the restroom for another human being, but I was quite alone. I thought about the Scripture, "My sheep know My voice" but I never expected the Shepherd's voice to be so firm. The tone of voice presented me with no option, and I caught up with the group just before the van left. This was my first experience in street ministry. Father knew best; it was what I needed; and after all, downtown Rome, New York, was not exactly New York City.

I Can Do This

The practical street experience gained at the seminar gave me slightly more confidence, so once back home, I started helping out with an outreach ministry in Rockefeller Center. The leader applied some pressure to volunteers to actually preach, but for the most part, new recruits could be productive by distributing tracts and fielding occasional inquiries. A few strangers did stop to talk, and I had to make eye contact; but I soon learned that even their negativity could sometimes be diffused by just listening and offering prayer if they were willing to accept. If not, I just became a target for their verbal wrath. Jesus had to deal with much more than that for my sake. There was a time when I was no longer considered a new recruit, and the time had come for my first sermon "al fresco." I gave my testimony—how God had delivered me from despair, suicidal thoughts, and alcohol and filled my life with the joy of His presence. Talking about the Lord and giving Him glory for His regenerative work was much easier to do than I had imagined. The major difficulty was physical—preaching without the aid of a microphone. My voice was just a rasp for three full days following. (Oh well, there went choir practice!)

Nip It in the Bud

I would like to say that all went well after breaking the ice and preaching my first sermon, but I cannot. It appeared that the honeymoon I enjoyed for many months was coming to an end. The byword for this next period of my life was "loss." First, the Bible school I attended closed. Of course I studied diligently on my own, but since I was preparing for church ministry, I needed to complete certification in the denominational school before I could teach or preach in the church. I also missed the fellowship of believers who were serious about serving

God. I traveled to classes with a young man from the church who became a good friend. He supervised an outreach coffeehouse connected with the church, which also was an enjoyable place to fellowship.

Loss number two happened when my friend, with whom I had attended the Bible school, suddenly married. It has always been my experience that maintaining a friendship with a man after he marries is detrimental to his relationship with his wife. Few women understand their husband having a female friend. As for me, I had no intention of marrying. My curt response was, "Why should I share my salary with a perfect stranger?" What I wanted was friendship, not romance!

These losses served to make me angry at God. I had prayed diligently about every situation, and it seemed that not one prayer was answered as I thought it should be. I had no idea this cycle of loss was just the beginning.

Counting the Cost

Continuing in street ministry became more costly for me. For many years, I competed for promotions in management in a technical area that had been exclusively a man's world. At that time, a woman had to excel in every area in order to win a promotion. A man could succeed even if he was quite average, as long as he had the right contacts. It was like a championship prize fight with a ten-point "must" system. Under this system a challenger had to unequivocally defeat the champion in order to win the title. Close calls always went in favor of the incumbent. Likewise, in the corporate world, unless a woman was completely superior in every aspect of the job, promotions and raises were given to the men. When things like my career, formerly so important to me, were stripped away, there was only one thing to do and that was to focus on serving Jesus.

On a day when I was just distributing tracts, my boss passed by. Identification with those in street ministry (generally not considered respectable or stable, like church ministers) proved to be corporate suicide for me. He seemed embarrassed but acknowledged me and accepted a tract. Soon after that, my career path was drastically reversed.

Projects I successfully had worked on for many months were removed from my portfolio and given to others. When there were no projects left for me to do, I was told I had to make a job for myself if I wanted to stay employed. I would like to think all this was suffering for the gospel's sake, but I cannot unequivocally make that link. My life's focus had changed from company business to the Father's business. One thing was certain, however: promotable company executives were not also lunchtime street preachers.

Coffeehouse Outreach Ministry

On Friday nights, I attended the Christian fellowship at a coffeehouse established to reach out to the surrounding community. This was a multiracial section of Queens, about a mile from the elevated subway trains. After worship, we would separate into groups of two and hit the streets with a stack of tracts and our Bibles, in hope of meeting someone the Lord had prepared to receive salvation.

My ministry partner was a young Puerto Rican man named Angelo. Angelo was barely out of his teens and did not understand that the street could be a dangerous place at night, especially for a woman alone. We walked about half a mile without much contact with other people, as this portion of the road went through a residential area where folks locked their doors tight at sundown. The only sign of life between the coffeehouse and the subway station was a pizza parlor. Just before reaching the pizza place, Angelo announced he was going to a different section, where people spoke Spanish. Before I could comment, off he went, leaving me alone and vulnerable. If he had waited only a few seconds more, he would have had many to speak to.

As if on cue, a gang of young men appeared and started to circle me as if I was lunch for hungry wolves. My experience growing up in the Bronx taught me the worst thing would be to show fear. I was still on a mission for the Lord, and if I was going to take a "beat-down," it would be for serving Him to the end. I whipped out my stack of gospel tracts and began handing them out to the startled young men, who obviously did not expect a noncombative yet aggressive response to their threatening behavior. The individual who appeared to be the leader of the pack glanced at the tract I gave him, laughed, and discarded, it saying something to his companions in Spanish that I did not understand. All I knew was that they abruptly went elsewhere. I knew the Lord had intervened on my behalf. I was inclined to believe I would be better off alone, without an Angelo type of partnership, and just trust the Lord. I may have harbored some anger toward the Lord, but I did trust in His protection.

The next major loss happened when the coffeehouse was completely closed off to me. The definition of purpose was changed from outreach group to men's fellowship, and since I was the only female involved ... well, sayonara, sister! Again, I felt disenfranchised. There was no alternative for me, as I had nothing in common with the women of the church. I was older than most, single, and not really a family person. It seemed the women's fellowship centered around husbands, children, crafts, and cooking, all of which held zero appeal for me. Frankly, I could not figure out what was going on. Everything good, comforting, and productive ended for me.

Another blow came on a hot day in August when I was again distributing literature in Manhattan at lunchtime. A burly young man approached, wearing a brightly colored tunic and a snood over his many braids. I reached out to hand him a tract, and he came up to me and slapped the entire stack out of my hands. His further attack was stopped when he lost his balance and then ran off when he saw others of our group approaching. I was not really injured, just shocked.

A worse experience was just ahead but not in the streets. One evening I received a phone call from a man I had not seen since Jesus changed my life. I started to tell him about the transformation in my life when he asked if he could come over to my house to hear more about it. I thought that was a great idea and had visions of leading him to the Lord. A short time after he arrived and finished his coffee, I began to tell him again how Jesus had really changed my entire life. A look came over his face that frightened me. I never had any reason to be afraid of this man, but in truth I did not know him all that well. I was just trying to capitalize on an opportunity to witness. I don't know whether it was always his intention or a demonic presence impelled him, but he attacked me, physically and sexually. I never had to deal with this kind of assault when I was a drunk and living a party lifestyle. How could God let this happen to me when I was doing His work? That was it! I was done. I didn't want to evict Jesus from my life, but I surely would not be doing any more outreach on the streets—or in my living room.

Common Sense Rules of the Kingdom

I hope my early experiences in evangelistic outreach have not frightened or discouraged you. These events demonstrate that serving in the kingdom is not without cost, nor is it without common-sense rules. My humiliation became valuable because I learned early that I could not do outreach my own way. I needed to heed the leading of the Holy Spirit in ministry and not lean to my own understanding (Prov. 3:5). There are rules for a reason. The Enemy will do all he can to immobilize potential workers as soon as they emerge, and I gave him a perfect opportunity. When Jesus sent out His disciples, they went out two by two. There were few examples of "lone wolf" ministry. I was within the will of God but not within the scope of His ways. I never took the time to pray about reaching out but was puffed up with my own eager desire to win a soul for Jesus. I got smarter quickly. It took a long time to overcome the humiliating assault. I needed to receive forgiveness from the Lord for my presumption before my heart could return to the task at hand. When I remembered the reason for outreach and the eternal destiny of the lost, my own suffering was put into proper perspective. I wanted to serve the Lord, and since the only pulpit open to me was the street, to the street I returned—with considerably less bravado.

The last episode of my work on the streets of Manhattan had a happier conclusion. My closest friends, Andrea and Leo, encouraged me to "suck it up" and resume street ministry in the Times Square area. This was an entirely different environment, more low-key, and under the direction of a young man recently arrived from California. He put no pressure on the Christians congregating at his ministry table. If anyone just wanted to stand there and fellowship with other believers, that was fine with him. I needed a less stressful place to gradually work back into outreach, and this seemed the ideal place to be. I had no hint of God's greater plan when I first walked up to his little table and viewed his display of gospel tracts. A few months later, that young man from California and I married. Over the next three years, a small church was born out of the street ministry. My ministry activities shifted from the street to the church, and I had the opportunity to teach the Bible every week. My husband and I continue to serve the Lord after more than thirty years of marriage. Although the nature of my ministry is primarily teaching, he is still in a form of street ministry. That is enough about me and my early experience. It is now time to talk about you.

A Place for You

Right now, you may be thinking that you have absolutely no call or interest in street ministry. This kind of outreach may not even be practical where you live because there is no place where numbers of people congregate. Street ministry is only one form of outreach. There are many different ways the Lord can use you to reach out to others with the gospel of Jesus Christ. You are unique, and there are people you can reach that others cannot. There is a place for you in making disciples for God's kingdom. In the following segments, we will examine different styles of evangelism, the personality traits that work well with each specific style, and the strengths and weaknesses to watch for.

There are several ways to describe the various styles of evangelism, but the approach I think is most practical is a division based on the individual personality traits best suited for each style. Every area is vital in reaching the lost for the kingdom, and no single approach is more powerful than another. It is important to realize this and not to consider any style less important than others. No matter which type of outreach fits you, you are called to help make disciples. There is a place for you to be used, according to the gifts the Lord has given you. There is a style where you will say, "I can do that!"

For the Kind and Compassionate

When you are part of the kingdom of God, it is hard to understand the very negative stereotypes about Christians created by the outside world. We are considered arrogant, aloof, judgmental, prideful, and self-righteous. Christians are viewed as out of touch with reality, old-fashioned, hypocritical, and just itchin' to force our beliefs and moral standards on others. We are perceived as "notch-cutters," making a cut on the handle of our six-shooter for each new convert made. We are never seen as simply loving the individual. The stereotypes alone cry out for real Christians who have a heart full of love and compassion to help change those negative images into a truer perception of who we really are. Enter the serving evangelist. These compassionate believers exhibit the fruit of the Holy Spirit (Gal. 5:22–23) in their personal lives and minister to real needs of others in very practical ways. They naturally notice needs that others do not see and find joy in meeting those needs.

Personality traits of kindness, goodness, and gentleness find their outlet in this venue. When these evangelists look at someone, they ask themselves, "How can I make life better for this person?" They are ready and willing to serve in the most humble ways, not seeking recognition, just gratified to alleviate suffering in others. Sometimes their kindness comes at substantial personal cost, and sacrifices of time and resources are commonplace. This is the person who volunteers to take a neighbor to the doctor and spend hours in the waiting room, encouraging and comforting. This is the one who brings groceries to a family who has lost their income, takes meals to the sick, and babysits for the mother who must attend to a hospitalized parent of her own. The opportunities are endless, and the mission field is all around us. Humility is a marked trait of this individual. In fact, these valued saints find it difficult to see themselves as "evangelists" at all. At best, this type of ministry paves the way for others to really "hear" the gospel because they have seen it in action. These humble, compassionate Christians illustrate by their actions the kindness and mercy of God.

However, there are some flags of warning to watch for. The most common pitfall of this style of ministry is that the focus becomes all works. We just never get around to sharing the gospel because we are fearful of risking the friendship. There is a difference between just being a good neighbor and being a servant of the Lord Jesus Christ. We must connect the practical service with the reason for that service; otherwise, what is the point? Remember that the point of service is always Jesus. We must always, always, always point to Jesus. That is our job, and this is something you can do no matter how shy you consider yourself. Remember that faith comes by hearing the Word of God (Rom. 10:14). Although words are no substitute for actions, actions are not a substitute for words either. The ministry field is on your doorstep. If not you, then who will tell them?

A biblical example of this ministry was seen in the life and death and life again of a woman from the town of Lydda. Tabitha, also known as Dorcas, was an example of someone engaged in practical, compassionate outreach (Acts 9:36–41). After her death, her neighbors made a point of showing her good works among them and sent for the apostle Peter, who just happened to be nearby. Tabitha was raised from the dead by his ministry.

> Now there was at Joppa a certain disciple named Tabitha, which by interpretation is called Dorcas: this woman was full of good works and almsdeeds which she did. And it came to pass in those days, that she was sick, and died: whom when they had washed, they laid her in an upper chamber. And forasmuch as Lydda was nigh to Joppa, and the disciples had heard that Peter was there, they sent unto him two men, desiring him that he would not delay to come to them. Then Peter arose and went with them. When he was come, they brought him into the upper chamber: and all the widows stood by him, weeping, and shewing the coats and garments which Dorcas made, while she was with them. But Peter put them all forth, and kneeled down, and prayed; and turning him to the body said, Tabitha, arise. And she opened her eyes: and when she saw Peter, she sat up. And he gave her his hand, and lifted her up, and when he had called the saints and widows, presented her alive. (Acts 9:36–41)

Dorcas was resurrected and given an even more dynamic testimony to add to her works of compassion. If Dorcas can show the love of Jesus Christ through the work of her hands, so can you!

For Those with Many Friends

If you love to have people gather at your home for activities and fellowship or just to sample the new recipe you or your spouse created, this area of evangelism is made for you. If you are open to inviting new acquaintances into your social circle, opportunity is literally knocking at your door. Let's start with the biblical example to further describe this kind of evangelism.

The gospel of Mark recounts Jesus's visit to Capernaum by the sea. I have had the pleasure of visiting Capernaum. It's a beautiful spot, and it is still possible to take a walk through the little town and see the foundations of the stone homes people lived in possibly in the time of Jesus. If I had to choose a place to live during the days of Jesus, Capernaum would be high on the list of my favorites. Built on the hillside, it was elevated high enough to enjoy a cool breeze coming off the Sea of Galilee. By our standards, the homes were very small and built close together, an advantage in this community because personal fellowship was an important part of daily life. However, there were those who were disqualified from fellowship with the socially acceptable "decent" folk. Among the excluded were the publicans or tax collectors who worked for the occupying Roman government.

If you were looking to make big bucks during the time of the Roman occupation, working as a tax collector was a way to achieve that end. The Romans had a certain sum that needed to be raised from the populace and sent to Rome. They did not instruct the tax collectors how much they could collect from individuals, only the amount they needed to pay to the government. The tax collector was not paid a salary, so his fees had to be added to the tax levied on the citizens, like a kind of vigorish. (Vigorish is the fee an illegal bookmaker charges clients to place a bet. Please don't ask me how I know such things.) The "vig" collected by Matthew and his fellow publicans was fluid and depended on what they estimated the taxpayer could afford. Anything could be taxable: a cart, a donkey, furniture, the catch of the day—just anything. Clearly, people engaged in such disloyal activities were not included on the A-list of the social roster in Capernaum or any other Jewish town.

Human fellowship is a basic need, and so tax collectors had little alternative but to congregate with others of like occupation, salted with a few other sinners also excluded from polite Jewish society. Such was the lot of a man called Levi, the son of Alphaeus. (That was his Jewish name, but in business, he was called Matthew.)

One day a very unusual type of rabbi came to town. He was certainly different than the Pharisees and was not intimidated by their attitude. In fact, He was not shy about confronting the Pharisees about their man-made rules craftily tacked on to the Law of Moses. Jesus walked past the station where Matthew was collecting revenue and said something shocking. This noted rabbi, with demonstrated healing powers, invited Matthew to follow Him. No way was Matthew going to miss this chance. He left everything—and I mean everything—to begin his new life as a follower of Rabbi Jesus of Nazareth. Jesus agreed to come to Matthew's home for a banquet that night, so Matthew had to hustle to get the banquet prepared and invite all the fellow members of the "society of the shunned." Oh yes, the Pharisees were invited to come too, if they wanted to.

Jesus established his willingness to break bread with needy souls. He would not recoil from the sinner but offered the services of the Great Physician, who could heal not only their bodies but also their souls. He demonstrated that He came to call sinners to repentance (Mark 2:15–17).

Thinking about Matthew and his friends, there is a lesson for outreach in our own times. When we invite people to our gatherings, do we cleanse the guest list so that only socially acceptable folk are included? Evangelism means outreach and the opportunity afforded a man with many friends is to bring others into the mix. Remember a prayer exercise in an earlier chapter in which you asked the Lord to show you who He was calling? Now's the time to activate your heart with that same prayer: "Lord, who among my acquaintances are you calling to repentance that I may seek him out and include him?" This kind of evangelism takes patience and perseverance, and those with many friends must not become easily discouraged. There is also a need to be guided by the Holy Spirit, because there are those who are not ready to listen and will become disruptive to the group. Stay close to the Lord in prayer and seek His guidance.

Other home gatherings where "prebelievers" may not feel too out of place is an "Ask the Teacher" party. If your church is blessed with someone who is spiritually trustworthy and knows the Word very well, you can invite that person as a special guest to give a short teaching in your home and then address Bible questions submitted in advance. This can be a kickoff social for a very productive Bible study and may draw those who have questions but would never go to a church. Don't blindside the teacher. Make sure all questions are written and submitted in advance. If you are a person with many friends, this is evangelism you can do!

There are some red flags to watch for in this style of evangelism. First of all, the host depends on someone else to deliver the gospel message and avoids direct delivery. This is an area where personal development is necessary. Also, the purpose of the gathering can be lost if the conversation degenerates to purely social chatter. It is imperative to keep the focus on Jesus. Once again, point to Jesus, point to Jesus, point to Jesus.

For the Socially Interactive (Invitational Style)

Maybe you're not the "host with the most," but you like to update people around you as to what is going on. You are probably a devotee of the news, keeping abreast of world situations and analyzing how events will impact the country or economy or legal system. When it comes to what's happening now, you are alert and aware.

This gift was evident in Bible times too. The generation into which Jesus was born was eagerly anticipating the coming of a Messiah. Of course, their concept of Messiah was millennia ahead of God's plan. All they really wanted to see was the defeat of the Romans and the kingdom of God immediately established, with the Jewish nation at its apex. This was the hope of every Jewish heart in the first century.

When Jesus first began public ministry by the Sea of Galilee, He was followed by two men who had been disciples of John the Baptist. Andrew scoped out the situation and brought a word-of-mouth report to his brother, Simon. Jesus took another walk through Galilee and met Philip. Philip probably had already heard of this rabbi because he lived in the same town as Andrew and Simon. When he met Jesus for himself, Philip sought out his best buddy, Nathanael, and told him they had found the promised Messiah, and his name was Jesus of Nazareth. Nathanael was typical of those who needed more than just a testimony to be convinced. He relied on what he knew experientially—that Jesus was from Nazareth, and Nazareth was not a prestigious place to come from. Why would God choose someone who came from Nazareth? (How could God use someone who came from the Bronx, or the south side of Chicago, or Watts … and on and on?) Jesus had to demonstrate, through supernatural means, that He was who Andrew and Simon and Philip proclaimed Him to be. Jesus described Nathanael's activities earlier that day, even his private prayer time. Nathanael believed and followed Jesus, changing all his earthly goals and his eternal destiny. The biblical example shows evangelism done one-on-one, by word of mouth, and it is the preferred method of communication for the socially active.

If you have a propensity to gossip, change that negative to a tool that serves God. Make sure the content of your conversation reports all the wonderful works of Jesus. Now that's news worth repeating!

A biblical example of someone who liked to spread the news is the Samaritan woman who Jesus met at the well. She was certainly a socially interactive person, and her gifts were used to spread the good news in her village. The lady had a hard life. We don't know the specific circumstances but she had married five times and now lived with a sixth man, to whom she was not married. Let's not judge her past, because Jesus didn't. We don't know her situation. She could have been widowed several times over and ended up with a man who would not give her a "get." This was the document of divorce issued by her husband, permitting her to remarry. If a man wanted to be vindictive, he just did not grant his wife a "get."

Jesus didn't pass up the woman of Samaria because of her shady past; instead, he reached out and offered her "living water." The Samaritan woman was well informed on issues beyond household tasks and certainly was not timid. She did not slither away when Jesus revealed her past and current sin. Because she believed Him to be a genuine prophet, she attempted to engage him in a political discussion, exploring a seminal question that divided Jews from Samaritans: "Where should God be worshipped?" Jesus not only answered her questions but revealed Himself directly to her as the Messiah. (If anyone ever tells you that Jesus never claimed to be the Messiah, send them to John 4:26.)

The woman could not contain her desire to spread the gospel at this point. She ran back to her village and said, "Come see a man who told me everything I ever did! Isn't He the Christ?" Because of her testimony, Jesus was invited to spend some time in town and many believed, not only because of the woman's word but because they had seen Jesus. The woman spread the news, told her story, and pointed to Jesus, who completed the work.

Think about your many friends and acquaintances. Think about the ones you need to introduce to the man who changed your life. You can do this!

For the Yarn-Spinner

A frequent character appearing in old-time cowboy movies was the older buckaroo who told interesting stories to illustrate a point. Some stories were long and drawn out, but most got the point across very well When Jesus spoke in parables, it was a form of yarn-spinning. He used familiar circumstances that were interesting to his audience to illustrate a theological point. Yarn-spinning can be an effective evangelism tool, especially if the people you are addressing need a gentler touch. When the story is told, it is often left up to the hearer to draw a conclusion. This is a very nonconfrontational way to make a point. The parables Jesus told had popular appeal because he used things that were familiar to the hearers. Not everyone in the crowds who followed Jesus understood the point of the parable, because spiritual things are discerned by spiritual means. The disciples often asked Jesus to explain, and so if you are a yarn-spinner, be prepared to offer an explanation of the point of your story. Creative people excel at this kind of evangelism. It is very important to consider your audience in using this technique. A pitfall of yarn-spinning is using illustrations that only partially show the point. No story outside of the Bible is perfect or complete, so it is important to think about what your yarn is actually portraying. It is also easy to get caught up in the story and get stuck in connecting it with Bible truths.

Nature is a great source for finding topics that relate to biblical truth. Jesus used wonderful expressions, like "consider the lilies of the field."

> And why take ye thought for raiment? Consider the lilies of the field, how they grow; they toil not, neither do they spin: And yet I say unto you, That even Solomon in all his glory was not arrayed like one of these. Wherefore, if God so clothe the grass of the field, which today is, and tomorrow is cast into the oven, shall he not much more clothe you, O ye of little faith? Therefore take no thought, saying, What shall we eat? or, What shall we drink? or, Wherewithal shall we be clothed? [For after all these things do the Gentiles seek:] for your heavenly Father knoweth that ye have need of all these things. But seek ye first the kingdom of God, and his righteousness; and all these things shall be added unto you. (Matt. 6:28–33)

The strength of yarn-spinning is that the point becomes memorable and is brought to mind when circumstances similar to your story are viewed. How many of us have been encouraged by the love of the father in the parable of the Prodigal Son, or moved to repentance with the publican who was so conscious of his own sin. We get a proper perspective on giving when we recall the story of the widow's mite. If you are a good storyteller, start building a repertoire of illustrations for anecdotes that will be meaningful to those seeking the Lord.

For the Deep Thinker and the Case-Maker

People who think of themselves as intellectuals probably will not respond to yarns, nor will they be particularly impressed with the cupcakes you bring to their homes. While they will enjoy the cupcakes, they will not likely alter their worldview because of the recipe. The expression "Different strokes for different folks" is certainly relative. For some, the use of logic, knowledge, and even just plain common sense form a powerful tool to reach others for Jesus. They speak to others through their minds. Intellectuals can be at a disadvantage if they allow reason to block the spiritual revelation by the Holy Spirit.

Our generation has been blessed with many notable apologists, those articulate and well-educated men and women who know how to make the case for the truth of Christianity. Many of these now-staunch believers were former atheists or agnostics who set out to study the Bible in order to prove it to be in error. The wonders of the Word of God never come back void, however, and once shown the truth in Scripture, many embrace Jesus Christ. You may recall J Warner Wallace, who worked as a cold-case detective in the city of Los Angeles who set out to disprove the resurrection of Jesus by using the same forensic techniques he applied to any other cold case. His conclusion was that if the same evidence for the resurrection reported in the Bible were used in a court of law, there would be no doubt that Jesus did indeed rise from the dead. That type of presentation will cause an intellect to want to listen to his case making. Since his conversion, Wallace has been used greatly as a "hot" case maker for the Lord.

A biblical example of someone with this gift is the apostle Paul. He was charged to bring the gospel to people who were not steeped in Jewish scripture and tradition. He had to find an alternate way to offer the gospel to Gentile cultures, different from the way the message was presented in the synagogues. Paul's journey brought him to the Greek city of Athens, a hub of culture and religion in the ancient world. Paul took a mental inventory of his surroundings and noticed idols dedicated to a plethora of pagan gods, including one to an unknown god. Paul used what was familiar to the Athenians to open a dialogue on Mars Hill. He attempted to introduce them to that unknown god in the person of Jesus Christ. His references included quotes of Greek poetry and reference to philosophies they would recognize. Paul searched for a key to unlock the intellectual barriers to receiving the gospel based on faith. Few Athenians were open to Paul's logic. They listened with some interest until he mentioned the resurrection of Jesus. Resurrection from the dead was something the Athenians could not accept. Believing that Christ rose from the dead is a matter of faith. Reason can block the work of the Spirit, and we know that no one can say that Jesus is Lord except by the Holy Spirit (1 Cor.12:3).

One pitfall of intellectual evangelism is getting so enmeshed in logic that the gospel is overlooked and not presented. For others, the approach can be overwhelming and confusing; in effect, blowing them out of the water. The beauty of God's Word is its simplicity, and it is still the work of the Father to draw men to Himself. If you are blessed with a keen mind and a willing spirit, case-making is certainly something you can do.

For the Observant and Extrovert

In God's cadre of outreach workers, some are just comfortable talking with all kinds of people from all kinds of cultures. A short description would be that these folks are just at ease. Outreach is as natural to their personalities as breathing, and they excel at turning any conversation to the topic of Jesus Christ. I know a missionary with this personality. He often greets complete strangers with, "I have a message for you from the Lord. He wants you to know He loves you very much." That sentence lays the groundwork for further conversation that will, at the very least, be memorable and positive. Another quality exemplified in at-ease people is they are very observant. The next opportunity for them to witness is always close at hand, and they expect people to respond positively. At-ease people take the initiative; they are direct but not confrontational. Their use of Scripture is clear and insightful, and there is an urgency to spread the Word of God. Peter and John, as we see them in the book of Acts, are examples of this type of evangelism.

A possible drawback might be a failure to meaningfully connect with the individual. Ministry is very general and short term and does not really speak to need. There is a focus on transferring information and not building an ongoing relationship. God has provisioned His army well. There are those who are called to minister to ongoing need, picking up where the at-ease person left off. Every personality is well suited to the work the Lord has called him or her to perform. If you are an easy communicator, start praying that the Lord will show you opportunities and open doors for outreach. You can do this.

For the Bold, Semibold, and Those the Lord Is Making Bold

There are those with a prophetic call on their lives who know they have a message from the Lord that must be delivered. This is a hard calling and those who exhibit it sometimes pay the price in personal relationships. It is a very confrontational call and can embody the worst possible stereotypes of outreach. There is a time and place for this type of evangelism. We see confrontation demonstrated in the message delivered by Peter in Acts 2. Peter, who just fifty days before, denied the Lord now stands in the midst of the crowds in Jerusalem, celebrating Pentecost. Peter doesn't hold back. He reminds them that they were culpable in the crucifixion of the Messiah (Acts 2:36). The result of directly confronting the sin: about three thousand were saved. Another biblical example is John the Baptist, who confronted sin in the priests, Levites, and even King Herod. Stephen rehearsed the history of Israel before confronting those who condemned him, calling them "stiff necked resisters of the Holy Ghost" (Acts 7:51). These three had two things in common: they confronted crowds, and they ultimately died a martyr's death.

This type of evangelism can be performed with grace, however, as demonstrated in our own time by Reverend Billy Graham. His messages follow a pattern, directly confronting sin and offering God's plan for salvation. If you have a confrontational message, it is imperative to remember that love must always be the motive for delivering it. Your message can be bold, clear, urgent, and direct but still not condemning and still cognizant of the feelings of others.

A major strength of the bold and semibold is the urgency of their message. These folks stand with sword in hand, willing to say hard things from which others recoil. They intuitively know the two-edged power of the Scripture sword, and respect the influence of the Word to bring correction. They hold people accountable, virtually demanding repentance and subsequent change. They will never be accused of beating around the bush, for directness is their watchword. The pitfall here is that the same element that is regarded as strength can also be the greatest weakness. That directness and urgency can cause them to ride roughshod over the emotions of others, and a harsh tone can undermine the work of the Holy Spirit. Bold people need to cultivate gentleness. If this describes you, you can be a John the Baptist in a Billy Graham suit if you will yield yourself to the same Word of God you wield and allow the fruit of the Spirit to be developed in you. You can achieve this because it is not really you doing the work but God. Submitting to God will allow you to function with His grace.

Testimony Evangelism

Every believer has a testimony, and your story can be an effective tool to win others to the Lord. God has created each of us as truly unique, but we are also much the same when it comes to emotions we experience. The details and circumstances of life may vary, but the hurts, loneliness, and disillusionment are feelings common to mankind. The strength of testimony evangelism is your story of how Jesus impacted your life. It's hard to argue with experience. There is a cost, however, to sharing your testimony. Making your story public means you will have to become vulnerable. Exposing your feelings opens the door to possible criticism, so it is important to treat your testimony as an offering to the Lord, to be used as He sees fit. Remember the end-time saints overcome by the "blood of the Lamb and the word of *their* testimony" (Rev.12:11).

In order to avoid the common pitfall of going off on a tangent and confusing your listeners, it is important to structure your testimony effectively. It is also wise to practice giving your testimony so that you can clearly tell your story without hesitation. The key is in keeping your testimony centered on Jesus and how He changed your life. An effective testimony doesn't have to be dramatic, but it has to be yours. Remember the testimony of the man born blind. He had confidence in his experience and boldly proclaimed, "One thing I know, that whereas I was blind, now I see" (John 9:25). This is something you can do, and with a little practice you will be effective.

Study/Teaching Outline for Yes, You Can!

The jobs not done yet!
- "He that winneth souls is wise" (Prov. 11:30).
    - Three tasks of the job of soul-winning: planting; watering; harvesting (1 Cor.3:6).
    - Most rewarding segment is partnering with God in the harvest, because we can see the fruit of labor.
    - Sharing your faith with others doesn't mean you will end up being the one to harvest.
    - You may be used of the Lord to just "plant a seed."
    - You may be the one to water the seed another has planted.
    - You may have the honor of harvesting and leading someone to the Lord.
- Each task is significant, and you will reap equal heavenly reward.
- Here's what Paul had to say about the process: "I have planted, Apollos watered; but God gave the increase. So then neither is he that planteth anything, neither he that watereth; but God that giveth the increase. Now he that planteth and he that watereth are one: and every man shall receive his own reward according to his own labor. For we are laborers together with

God: ye are God's husbandry, ye are God's building"(1 Cor. 3:6–9).

- Don't be discouraged if you don't see the fruit of your soul-winning.
- In all things remember, "We walk by faith not by sight" (2 Cor. 5:7).

A place for you
- There are different styles of seed planting and watering.
- Certain personality traits function more effectively within selected types.
- There are strengths and weaknesses typical of each style of evangelism.
- Look for a biblical example of each type.
  ◦ Your personality does not lock you into a particular style of evangelism.
  ◦ You can still be used by the Lord in any type, regardless of your personality.
- Each area is as vital in reaching the lost as any other area. No style is less important, and all are needed to make disciples.

For the kind and compassionate
- Mercy in action. This style overcomes negative stereotypes about Christians.
- Qualities of the kind and compassionate person:
  ◦ Minister to real needs in practical ways
  ◦ Spots needs others miss
  ◦ Thought pattern: "How can I make life better for this person?"
  ◦ Willing to serve in humble ways; not seeking recognition
- Strength: paves the way for hearing the gospel because gospel has been demonstrated in action.
  ◦ Acts of service affect even the hardest-to-reach people.
  ◦ Loving service is both hard to resist and difficult to argue with.

- Weaknesses: making it clear to others why you are serving them.
- Be careful not to impose your service on others.
  - Don't persist in being helpful whether they want it or not. (This is called becoming a nuisance.)
  - Pray for wisdom to know where to invest your efforts in ways that will be strategic for the kingdom of God.
- A common failing is in never getting around to the reason for your service. Faith comes by hearing.
  - Remember that although words are no substitute for actions, actions are no substitute for words either (Rom. 10:14). Paul says that we must verbally tell people about Christ.
  - Your acts of kindness will be attributed to other causes (for example, what a good person you are) and even other religions if you do not make it clear *who* it is *you* serve.
- Biblical examples of kind and compassionate service evangelism
  - Tabitha (also known as Dorcas) was always doing good and helping the poor. She was well known for her loving acts of service performed in the name of Christ. She was even called a disciple (Acts 9:36).

Suggestions for developing a dynamic serving style of evangelism.
- Be deliberate in communicating the spiritual motivation behind your acts of service. It could be through a word, a card, or an invitation.
- Pray for openings to serve and to speak about Jesus to others. He will open your eyes to areas you might have missed. Be ready to follow His leadings, even if they seem unusual.
- For those with many friends
  - Friendship evangelism: building relationships with the unsaved
  - Expanding your circle of friends to include the unsaved
  - This style takes patience and perseverance. (Expect invitations to be refused, but be persistent.)
  - Seek the Lord for insight as to who to invite into the circle of friends. (Those who are not ready can become a disruptive influence.)

- Strengths: keeping in contact with the lost so as to reach them for Christ.
  ○ Paul strove to be "all things to all people" (1 Cor. 9:19–23).
- Pitfalls: it is easy to value friendship over truth.
  ○ Telling people they are sinners in need of a Savior will test relationships. (It is easy to avoid risking the relationship.)
  ○ It is easy to wait too long and avoid what is the ultimate goal: bringing people to know Christ as Savior and Lord.
- Biblical example of friendship evangelism: Levi the tax collector became Matthew the disciple.
  Matthew invited his former coworkers to come and meet Jesus. And as Jesus passed forth from thence, he saw a man, named Matthew, sitting at the receipt of custom: and he saith unto him, Follow me. And he arose, and followed him. And it came to pass, as Jesus sat at meat in the house, behold, many publicans and sinners came and sat down with him and his disciples. And when the Pharisees saw it, they said unto his disciples, Why eateth your Master with publicans and sinners? But when Jesus heard that, he said unto them, They that be whole need not a physician, but they that are sick. But go ye and learn what that meaneth, I will have mercy, and not sacrifice: for I am not come to call the righteous, but sinners to repentance. (Matt. 9:9–13)
- Some suggestions on how to accomplish friendship evangelism.
  ○ Be patient. This style tends to work more gradually than others. Look and pray for opportunities to turn conversations toward spiritual matters.
  ○ Continually create and plan opportunities to interact with friends and new people through social events, sports, etc.
  ○ Practice telling the gospel message so you will be prepared when the opportunity arises.
- For the socially interactive:
  ○ Invite others to go with you to places and events where Jesus Christ is taught.
  ○ Those who are aware of what is going on in the community excel here. These are the "happening" people.

- ○ Biblical examples:
  - ▪ Jesus's first disciples—word-of-mouth evangelism (John 1). "Come and see."
  - ▪ The Samaritan woman went back to her village and simple invited the people saying, "Come, see a man, which told me all things that ever I did: is not this the Christ? Then they went out of the city, and came unto him" (John 4:29–30).
  - ▪ Modern example: inviting others to a gospel crusade, special evangelistic church event, or an invitation to hear someone's testimony
- The yarn-spinner
  - ○ People who excel at telling or creating a story.
  - ○ Using familiar circumstances to illustrate a theological point.
  - ○ Biblical example: the parables of Jesus
  - ○ The hearers are led to draw a conclusion.
- Strengths
  - ○ This is a gentle and nonconfrontational way to make a point.
  - ○ Memorable way of making the point. People remember the stories.
- Weakness
  - ○ Not everybody can draw the intended conclusion.
  - ○ Requires knowledge of the audience.
  - ○ No illustration outside of the Bible can be complete; partial illustration.
  - ○ Can get caught up in the story and fail to connect it with the spiritual point.
- Understanding spiritual things requires the working of the Holy Spirit.
  - ○ Suggestion: Start building a repertoire of illustrations and anecdotes that will meaningfully illustrate the need for salvation, the path to follow, etc.

- For the deep thinker and the case-maker
  - The use of logic, knowledge, and common sense to win people to Jesus.
  - Intellectuals require an appeal through the mind.
  - This style is best for people who can discuss analytical issues, such as doctrine, philosophy, and science.
    - (The fishing is good at universities and among professionals of various kinds.)
  - This type of evangelist is known as a "Christian apologist." An "apologist" is someone who defends or supports a position that may be controversial.
    - Requires skill in rightly dividing the Word of God (2 Tim. 2:15)
    - Skill in making and communicating the case for Christianity
  - Several well-known Christian apologists were former atheists.
- Biblical example of an apologist is the apostle Paul:
  - His credentials: "Though I might also have confidence in the flesh. If any other man thinketh that he hath whereof he might trust in the flesh, I more: Circumcised the eighth day, of the stock of Israel, of the tribe of Benjamin, an Hebrew of the Hebrews; as touching the law, a Pharisee; Concerning zeal, persecuting the church; touching the righteousness which is in the law, blameless. But what things were gain to me, those I counted loss for Christ" (Phil. 3:4–7).
  - Paul had the best education possible. "I am verily a man which am a Jew, born in Tarsus, a city in Cilicia, yet brought up in this city at the feet of Gamaliel, and taught according to the perfect manner of the law of the fathers, and was zealous toward God, as ye all are this day" (Acts 22:3).
  - Paul's resolve: keep it simple! "For I determined not to know anything among you, save Jesus Christ, and him crucified" (1 Cor. 2:2).

- Strengths: knowledge and ability to reach many different cultures.
- Weakness: reason can block the work of the Holy Spirit. Things of the Spirit are spiritually discerned (1 Cor.12:3).
  ○ Can get so enmeshed in the broad logic that the simple gospel is overlooked
  ○ Can get focused on a specific point, becoming an "expert" in this area that has little to do with the simple gospel
  ○ Straying from the simplicity of the gospel of Christ
- For the observant and extrovert
  ○ People with an easy manner of speaking to people.
  ○ Outreach is natural to their personality.
  ○ Usually very observant, looking for opportunities to share the gospel.
  ○ They take the initiative.
  ○ They expect people to respond positively.
- Strengths: direct approach but nonconfrontational
  ○ Insightful use of Scripture
  ○ Usually conveys an urgency to the salvation message
- Weakness: does not really connect with people or address specific need.
  ○ Transfers information but does not build relationship; short-term ministry.
- Biblical examples: Peter and John working together in the book of Acts exemplify an easy communication style (Acts 3:6).
- For the bold, semibold, and those the Lord is making bold
  ○ People with a burning message from the Lord that *must* be delivered.
  ○ This style of evangelism generally targets a mass assembly of people, not individuals.
  ○ Message, at best, confronts sin and is followed by the plan of salvation but can also reference coming judgment.
- Strengths: message is clear, direct, and urgent.
  ○ People are held accountable.
  ○ Repentance is required.

- Weaknesses: this is the kind of evangelism most of us "love to hate."
  - The speaker is exposed, not usually in the protective environment of home or church.
  - Church people do not understand confrontational behavior or zeal, and so isolation from the rest of the body of Christ is a common pitfall for the confrontational evangelist.
  - The boldness that is considered "a strength" can also ride roughshod over people's feelings.
- Biblical examples: Peter confronts the Jews of Jerusalem (Acts 2:14–37).
  - He confronts their mocking.
    "But Peter, standing up with the eleven, lifted up his voice, and said unto them, Ye men of Judaea, and all ye that dwell at Jerusalem, be this known unto you, and hearken to my words: For these are not drunken, as ye suppose, seeing it is but the third hour of the day" (Acts 2:14–15).
  - He plants seed: fulfillment of familiar prophecy
    But this is that which was spoken by the prophet Joel; And it shall come to pass in the last days, saith God, I will pour out of my Spirit upon all flesh: and your sons and your daughters shall prophesy, and your young men shall see visions, and your old men shall dream dreams: And on my servants and on my handmaidens I will pour out in those days of my Spirit; and they shall prophesy: And I will shew wonders in heaven above, and signs in the earth beneath; blood, and fire, and vapour of smoke: The sun shall be turned into darkness, and the moon into blood, before the great and notable day of the Lord come. (Acts 2:16–20)
  - He waters the promise of salvation given by Joel. "And it shall come to pass, that whosoever shall call on the name of the Lord shall be saved" (Joel 2:32).
  - Peter Confronts their sin. "Ye men of Israel, hear these words; Jesus of Nazareth, a man approved of God among you by miracles and wonders and signs, which God did

by him in the midst of you, as ye yourselves also know: Him, being delivered by the determinate counsel and foreknowledge of God, ye have taken, and by wicked hands have crucified and slain: ... This Jesus hath God raised up, whereof we all are witnesses. Therefore being by the right hand of God exalted, and having received of the Father the promise of the Holy Ghost, he hath shed forth this, which ye now see and hear" (Acts 2:22–23, 32–33).

- ◦ Peter makes it plain who Jesus is: "Therefore let all the house of Israel know assuredly, that God hath made the same Jesus, whom ye have crucified, both Lord and Christ" (Acts 2:36).

- ◦ Peter's confrontational style reaps a large harvest. "Now when they heard this, they were pricked in their heart, and said unto Peter and to the rest of the apostles, Men and brethren, what shall we do? Then Peter said unto them, Repent, and be baptized every one of you in the name of Jesus Christ for the remission of sins, and ye shall receive the gift of the Holy Ghost ... Then they that gladly received his word were baptized: and the same day there were added unto them about three thousand souls." (Acts 2:37–38, 41).

- Remember, different bait works for different fish.
  - ◦ Many styles of outreach for many different people.
  - ◦ Just because this style may not be for you, beware of criticizing what God is doing through others.
  - ◦ As long as they are preaching the Lord, they are seeding and watering. "And John answered and said, Master, we saw one casting out devils in thy name; and we forbad him, because he followeth not with us. And Jesus said unto him, Forbid him not: for he that is not against us is for us" (Luke 9:49–50).

- Testimony evangelism: "That which was from the beginning, which we have heard, which we have seen with our eyes, which we have looked upon, and our hands have handled, of the Word of life; [For the life was manifested, and we have seen it, and bear witness, and shew unto you that eternal life, which was with the Father, and was manifested unto us;] That which we have seen and heard declare we unto you, that ye also may have fellowship with us: and truly our fellowship is with the Father, and with his Son Jesus Christ" (1 John 1:1–3).

- ○ Every believer has a testimony that can be a soul-winning tool.
- ○ Your story is unique but many can relate to your circumstances.

- Strengths: This is your experience, how Jesus affected your life. It is hard to argue with personal experience. Remember saints overcome by the blood of the Lamb and the word of their testimonies (Rev. 12:11).
  - ○ Cost of sharing your testimony: becoming vulnerable about personal life.
- Weaknesses: "tangent talking," something meaningful to you but not relative to the one you are talking to.
- Giving your testimony effectively, especially to an individual, means being a good listener. *Listen* first and then determine how your experience relates.
  - ○ Don't discount your own testimony because it seems ordinary. Ordinary stories relate to ordinary people, and we are all basically ordinary people.
  - ○ Taking it further: don't stop with just telling your story. Challenge your listener to consider how your testimony might apply to his own life.
  - ○ Construct your testimony in an effective way.
  - ○ Practice so you will be able to tell your story without hesitation.
  - ○ Keep Christ and His message as the centerpiece (how He changed your life).
  - ○ Keep your story fresh by adding current illustrations from your ongoing walk with Christ.
  - ○ An effective testimony doesn't have to be dramatic but it has to be yours.

- Biblical example of testimony evangelism: the man born blind (John 9).
  - He'd been blind since birth and regularly sat begging from passing people. His routine quickly changed when Jesus gave him the gift of sight.
  - No sooner was he healed than he was brought in front of a hostile audience and asked to explain what had happened.
  - The man refused to enter into theological debate with them (John 9:25).
    - Paul would have been happy to oblige and give them a few scriptural arguments, and Peter would have confronted their hypocrisy.
    - Those responses didn't fit who this man was. He just told what he knew.
    - He had confidence in his testimony: "One thing I do know. I was blind but now I see!"
    - Even the learned and powerful could not argue with his testimony. This man was *born blind*. God prepared this man all of his life for his testimony, and he told it in a way that would point people toward Christ.
    "And his disciples asked him, saying, Master, who did sin, this man, or his parents, that he was born blind? Jesus answered, Neither hath this man sinned, nor his parents: but that the works of God should be made manifest in him" (John 9:2–3).

Prayer—the starting point for all types of evangelism
- Tune in to the work of the Holy Spirit.
  - Become sensitive to the Holy Spirit when you pray.
  - Even Jesus didn't make a move until He observed what the Father was doing. "Then answered Jesus and said unto them, Verily, verily, I say unto you, The Son can do nothing of himself, but what he seeth the Father do: for what things soever he doeth, these also doeth the Son likewise" (John 5:19).
  "For I have not spoken of myself; but the Father which sent me, he gave me a commandment, what I should say, and

what I should speak. And I know that his commandment is life everlasting: whatsoever I speak therefore, even as the Father said unto me, so I speak" (John 12:49–50).

- *Listen!* Prayer time becomes intercessory prayer.
  - ○ Who is the Lord bringing to mind in your prayer?
  - ○ Ask the Lord to reveal who (in your circle of influence) He is drawing.
  - ○ Ask the Lord to reveal the needs of that person; then pray for him or her.
  - ○ Ask the Lord to show you your current interaction with that person.
  - ○ Pray for an opening to share your faith with this individual.

CHAPTER SIX

Tell It Like It Is
(Constructing an Effective Testimony)

"Whosoever therefore shall confess me before men, him will I confess also before my Father which is in heaven" (Matt. 10:32).

In a court of law, cases are tried and judged based on many elements. Foremost among them will be physical evidence and witness testimony. When a witness takes the stand, you can be sure that the attorney calling for the testimony has carefully prepared the witness and has developed questions that will elicit the information needed to prove his point. The testimony will be structured to keep the speaker on track and to avoid extraneous information that would only serve to confuse the jury. Likewise, the opposing attorney will listen carefully, having familiarized herself with what the witness might say. She will also have prepared additional questions to steer the witness and mitigate any possible impact to her case. I can't imagine a credible attorney would risk an impromptu testimony in a court trial if it could be avoided. Likewise, a wise believer will prepare his testimony with care in order to glorify the Lord in an accurate and concise manner.

Every believer has a testimony, and your personal witness statement is a powerful evangelistic tool. Of course, we want to tell it like it is, accurately and without embellishment, relying on the anointing of the Holy Spirit. Don't be concerned that careful preparation will in anyway diminish the power of the Holy Spirit's speaking through you. If anything, preparation and practice will sharpen the impact of communicating the wonderful work God has done in you. Also, when your testimony is well prepared, your level of confidence will increase. You will find yourself not only ready but eager to share the changes brought about by God in your life when you are called upon to deliver your story. Structuring your testimony is no different from any other undertaking; it must begin with prayer. Ask the Lord to clear your mind and help you put your experience into words that will honor and glorify Him.

Basic Guidelines

Most experts in giving effective testimonies advocate formatting your story into four parts, answering four basic questions:

1. What was your life like before you came to know Jesus?
2. What happened in your life to make you realize you needed a Savior?
3. How did you actually receive Jesus?
4. How has Jesus made your life full and meaningful?

Notice that the first three questions concern your life BC (before Christ). Be careful that you do not get trapped in majoring on your evil past. A detailed rendition of your life of sin does not glorify God and will result in the wrong focus. Watch the details. If you plan on limiting your entire testimony to about three minutes, the brevity required to answer the four questions will be apparent. Your testimony should be short, simple, pointed, and positive, and achieving this is not a simple task. It will take some work. I suggest you write it out and practice delivering it. The more you prepare, the more confident you will be.

Not every testimony will involve the salvation experience. There are many who were born under the third pew and subsequently raised in church nursery. These people never strayed from moral Christian behavior even into adulthood. You may not be able to point to a specific moment in time when you surrendered your life to Jesus. Look for an event that brought you closer to the Lord. What caused you to realize you needed to recommit your life and labor to Him? How has your life changed since you recommitted? You have a testimony too. Pray for the leading of the Lord to recall the circumstances that can be best used in outreach. Church folk need to be reached too. There are many who have lost the passion they once had and like the people of the church of Ephesus mentioned in Revelation, they need to be encouraged to rediscover their "first love" (Rev.2:1–7). Be creative in identifying three or four questions around which you can build your testimony.

There are some helpful pointers to remember in building your testimony, whether it is about salvation or Christian growth. It is helpful to be aware of the background and experience of your audience. Addressing a Bible school dropout who's familiar with Scripture will likely be quite different from talking to your next-door neighbor who has carefully avoided anything resembling a church. No matter the skill of your listeners, it is a good idea to keep it simple and stick to the point. Assess your listeners and try to find a point in your story with which they will identify. Avoid using language terms that are esoteric, understood by churchgoers but few others. This can cause them to tune out and destroy the possibility of their identifying with your story. For example, do not pack your story with words like born-again, saved, lost, repent, gospel, or sin. Try to find words that convey the same idea but are more easily understood by a general audience. When you want to say born-again, you might use something like, "I was given a new spiritual life." For the big buzz word, sin, you might use "a crime against God's law" or "rejecting God." Work on the exact thought you want to convey in your message. Translate "Christian-ese" into familiar and easily understood concepts.

It is a good idea to secure permission from your listeners to speak to them about your spiritual experience. One frequent criticism of Christians is that we force our beliefs on others. If you secure permission, this objection is satisfied.

A big no-no in giving your testimony is addressing divisive doctrines. Arguing theology is not the point of your story, and debating such things as the merits of a specific method of baptism is irrelevant to someone who is not saved. Never cast a specific church or individual minister in a negative light. That will load the Enemy's cannon and take over the spotlight, destroying focus that must be on the Lord.

Let's do a little fun exercise here. The following is an example of a very poor testimony. Next to each line, you get to make a comment. What is wrong or right with the statement? (Discussion questions will follow.)

Example of a Poorly Constructed Testimony	**Your Comment**

My Life before Jesus

I just want to say a few things about the Second Street Church and _____

Pastor Ryan. He really got to me when he said that I had to be _____

baptized all over again because I was baptized as a baby, and I _____

really didn't know anything about Jesus then. The rest of the _____

people in the church didn't believe I was saved because I wasn't _____

baptized by being dunked, but I was sprinkled when I was a baby. _____

I was really hurt by Pastor Ryan and the other people too. I think _____

they are hypocrites. They didn't show me love like the Bible _____

says they should. I have been hurt all my life. I was born and raised _____

in Wheaton, Illinois, with two brothers and a couple of sisters who _____

didn't like me either. High school was a horror show, and I _____

didn't make any friends because nobody wanted to hang around _____

with me. My family went to church all
the time; every time the doors

were open, my mother went to church.
She left me alone, and

I don't think she liked me very much
either. I think she was a

hypocrite too. After high school I
decided to get even with

everyone who hated me, and so I started
to drink alcohol and

party with a crowd that used drugs and
did other things too.

I wasn't as bad as they were because I
only used alcohol and not drugs.

Soon, I had a few boyfriends, but I had
to share them with other girls.

At least they liked me until I got
pregnant, but at least they liked me.

How I Met Jesus

Then I came to your church, and the
people were nice to me.

So I stopped drinking and sleeping
around. The preacher told

me I had to accept Jesus as my Savior or
I would end up in hell.

I didn't want to go to hell, so I said this
prayer and now I am saved.

Glory to God, hallelujah!

My Life Since

My life is better now. Praise Jesus! Glory
to God!

I don't drink as much as before, and I
only have one boyfriend. _____

I hope he is my baby's daddy. I really
don't know for sure. _____

Discussion Questions:
1. Compare the above testimony to the basic guidelines.
2. Does this testimony glorify God? If not, who is glorified?
3. If you belonged to this church, how would you help this young woman?

A Very Good Testimony, Given Twice

The book of Acts records the conversion testimony of the apostle Paul, given on two separate occasions, in two separate chapters. Although in each situation his circumstances were dangerous, his story and delivery was powerful and compelling. A close look at Paul's words demonstrates that he utilized elements we cited under the topic of "basic structure."

In the twenty-second chapter of the book of Acts, Paul was the target of violence perpetrated by a Jerusalem mob, inspired by religious Jews visiting from Asia. He was accused of teaching against the law and bringing Gentiles into restricted areas of the temple. The mob sought to kill him, seizing and dragging him out of the temple, presumably toward a place of execution. Were it not for God's intervention, through the interception of the Roman commander, the mob might have succeeded. Talk about a tough audience! Paul asked and received permission from the Roman commander to address the mob. Paul knew his listeners were behaving as zealous Jews, an attitude very familiar to the apostle. He directed his testimony specifically to this group by giving his testimony in the Hebrew language instead of the Greek language, which was commonly used for everyday business. Since he was addressing those who thought they were doing God's work by defending Judaism, Paul attempted to have the crowd identify with his experience through his own exceptional religious background.

He began his story by citing his credentials and relating the account of his life before he met Jesus, when he ferociously persecuted Christians to prison and to death. He appealed to the accepted Hebrew authority for verification in stating that even the high priest could attest to both his background and zealousness. Scripture does not record how the crowd reacted to his statements, so we do not know if Paul's attempt to find an area of identification had an effect. Paul continued his story, dramatically describing how he met Jesus on the road to Damascus and how he was directed to go into the city and wait for further instructions. Still, we do not know how the crowd responded to his miraculous encounter with Jesus. Paul went on to cite his life circumstances, both immediately after his conversion and after he returned to Jerusalem. The mob listened attentively to Paul's testimony until he struck a nerve. They could not accept that God sent him to the Gentiles (Acts 22:21–22). The violent response of the crowd who called for Paul's death resulted in his being taken into custody by the Roman authority.

In briefly reviewing the pattern Paul followed, we see that he asked and received permission to speak, assessed his listening audience, and attempted to create identification points. He then told of his life before Jesus, identified the circumstances of his conversion, and spoke of the directional change in his life. Paul told it like it was, even if the response was not what he desired. Actually, his arrest by the Romans eventually set up the second opportunity to tell of his conversion, recorded a few chapters later in Acts 26.

The Saga Continues

Following his violent confrontation with the Jews in Jerusalem, Paul was brought to the Roman city of Caesarea, where he was called to testify before Felix, the governor. After two years of waiting, he was summoned by the new governor, Festus, who wanted to clear up cases held over from the previous administration. He was surprised to find that Paul had not been accused of any offense against Rome but had been charged with religious transgressions involving his belief in a man he taught was the Jewish Messiah. Festus logically determined that a charge brought by Jews against a Jew, alleging an offense against Jewish traditions, ought to be tried in a Jewish court, but Paul refused to be transported back to Jerusalem, since certain death awaited him there. Paul exercised his right as a Roman citizen to be heard before the Roman emperor. Jurisdiction was now transferred from Festus at Caesarea to Augustus in Rome. The change of venue presented only one further duty for Festus: what should he write to Augustus concerning the charges against Paul? Festus was newly appointed to the governorship and, as such, received a courtesy visit from the reigning king, Agrippa II, who was also a Roman appointee. Festus took the opportunity to elicit help from Agrippa in preparing his communication to Caesar.

When Agrippa II heard Paul's saga, he requested an opportunity to examine the man the Jews were so intent on destroying. These are the circumstances surrounding the second recorded testimony of Paul the apostle.

Assessing the Listener(s)

Paul was intelligent and well educated, so it is safe to assume that he also was well acquainted with history in Israel, including the pedigree of the king. Agrippa II was the great-grandson of Herod the Great, the builder of the temple in Jerusalem and the man who issued the edict to destroy the infant boys of Bethlehem following Jesus's birth. Although Herod the Great was a descendant of Esau and technically not a Jew, the Romans determined his pedigree was close enough for government work. He was appointed by the Roman senate to be king over the nation of Israel. When Herod the Great died, he divided his kingdom and kingdom authority into four parts, to be assigned to his sons. His son Herod Antipas was called Herod the Tetrarch, reflecting that he ruled over a quarter share of the kingdom. His domain centered in Galilee. Herod Antipas is notorious for the murder of John the Baptist and was the king involved in the trial and crucifixion of Jesus. The entire Herodian clan of monarchs would be an easy choice for inclusion in the top-ten list of "Bad Boys of the Bible." The ungodly family stream continued with the reign of Herod Agrippa I. He persecuted the early church in Jerusalem and had the apostle James executed (and attempted to do the same to Peter). Agrippa I died suddenly and in a humiliating manner when he accepted acclamation as a god. The Bible records that an angel of the Lord struck him, and he died, being eaten by worms (Acts 12:21–23). His son, Herod Agrippa II, is the man who assisted Festus in hearing Paul. He was raised in Rome but was very familiar with the law and traditions of the Jews. Paul likely would have been familiar with all these facts, except that Agrippa II would be the last of Herod's dynasty.

It is probable that Paul gave his testimony hundreds of times to different groups of people with differing backgrounds. I can't imagine that he would not have shared his story multiple times with each church he visited. Tailoring the testimony to the audience was essential in his appearance before Festus and Agrippa II. The following Scripture demonstrates how Paul, after receiving permission to speak, assessed the hearers and tried to find a link to enable them to connect with the wondrous event that changed Saul of Tarsus into Paul, the apostle of Jesus Christ.

Paul receives permission, assesses his audience, and reaches out with positive affirmation. "Then Agrippa said to Paul, 'You have permission to speak for yourself.' So Paul motioned with his hand and began his defense: 'King Agrippa, I consider myself fortunate to stand before you today as I make my defense against all the accusations of the Jews, and especially so because you are well acquainted with all the Jewish customs and controversies. Therefore, I beg you to listen to me patiently'" (Acts 26:1–3 NIV).

Paul Describes His Life before Meeting Jesus

"The Jewish people all know the way I have lived ever since I was a child, from the beginning of my life in my own country, and also in Jerusalem. They have known me for a long time and can testify, if they are willing, that I conformed to the strictest sect of our religion, living as a Pharisee" (Acts 26:4–5 NIV).

(Note: Paul raises a controversy, but the king was surely familiar with this debate. It was not a divisive issue for Agrippa.)

"And now it is because of my hope in what God has promised our ancestors that I am on trial today. This is the promise our twelve tribes are hoping to see fulfilled as they earnestly serve God day and night. King Agrippa, it is because of this hope that these Jews are accusing me. Why should any of you consider it incredible that God raises the dead?" (Acts 26:6–8 NIV).

Paul Shares His Personal Thoughts and Reasoning Prior to Meeting Jesus

"I too was convinced that I ought to do all that was possible to oppose the name of Jesus of Nazareth. And that is just what I did in Jerusalem. On the authority of the chief priests I put many of the Lord's people in prison, and when they were put to death, I cast my vote against them. Many a time I went from one synagogue to another to have them punished, and I tried to force them to blaspheme. I was so obsessed with persecuting them that I even hunted them down in foreign cities" (Acts 26:9–12 NIV).

Details of the Events That Changed His Thinking and Behavior

> On one of these journeys I was going to Damascus with the authority and commission of the chief priests. About noon, King Agrippa, as I was on the road, I saw a light from heaven, brighter than the sun, blazing around me and my companions. We all fell to the ground, and I heard a voice saying to me in Aramaic, "Saul, Saul, why do you persecute me? It is hard for you to kick against the goads." Then I asked, "Who are you, Lord?" "I am Jesus, whom you are persecuting," the Lord replied. "Now get up and stand on your feet. I have appeared to you to appoint you as a servant and as a witness of

what you have seen and will see of me. I will rescue
you from your own people and from the Gentiles. I am
sending you to them to open their eyes and turn them
from darkness to light, and from the power of Satan to
God, so that they may receive forgiveness of sins and a
place among those who are sanctified by faith in me."
(Acts 26:12–18 NIV)

What His Life Is Like Now

So then, King Agrippa, I was not disobedient to the
vision from heaven. First to those in Damascus, then
to those in Jerusalem and in all Judea, and then to the
Gentiles, I preached that they should repent and turn to
God and demonstrate their repentance by their deeds.
That is why some Jews seized me in the temple courts
and tried to kill me. But God has helped me to this
very day; so I stand here and testify to small and great
alike. I am saying nothing beyond what the prophets
and Moses said would happen—that the Messiah would
suffer and, as the first to rise from the dead, would
bring the message of light to his own people and to the
Gentiles. (Acts 26:19–23 NIV)

Constructing Your Testimony—How to Begin

Paul's journey from persecutor to liberator, which followed his
miraculous meeting with Jesus, began with the first obedient steps
taken toward Damascus. Notice that he was blind. Right now, you
may feel you are blind too, not seeing clearly the events in your life
that can be best used by the Lord in evangelism. Remember that every
journey begins with prayer. Paul spent three days in darkness, praying
and fasting, before the Lord sent Ananias to restore his sight.

The apostle John frequently referred to the fact that he was an
eyewitness to the events about which he testified. In his first epistle,

John speaks about the things he saw and heard and even handled, with the intent that the reader would be able to fellowship with the believers. What firsthand experiences have you had that will encourage others to fellowship with the Father, Son, and Holy Spirit?

Worksheet/Guidelines for Constructing Your Testimony

General Guidelines for Being Concise and Effective

- Keep it simple and brief. (If it's too long, hearers will lose interest.)
- Be aware of your audience background.
- Avoid "Christian-ese" language—terms like born-again, saved, repent. (Find words reflecting the same meaning to which your hearer can relate.)
- Don't specifically reference churches or ministers in a negative light.
- Stick to the point. Check your testimony for distracting details. (It's all about Jesus and what He did in your life.)
- Don't address divisive doctrinal issues (for example, baptism style, predestination).
- Be truthful, and don't exaggerate. Share your true feelings.
- Share how Jesus changed your life. (Always focus on Him.)
- Avoid talking about your past sins in great detail. (This does not glorify the Lord.)

Testimony Worksheet

- What Was My Life Like Before I Met Jesus Christ?

- How I Met Jesus Christ

- How Has My Life Changed Since Accepting Jesus Christ?

- What Is My Life Like Now?

CHAPTER SEVEN

Let This Sink Down in Your Ears

"**A**nd they were all amazed at the mighty power of God. But while they wondered everyone at all things which Jesus did, he said unto his disciples, Let these sayings sink down into your ears: for the Son of man shall be delivered into the hands of men" (Luke 9:43–44).

Jesus needed His followers to really hear Him, but they obviously were experiencing a "disconnect" between the miracles they witnessed and the words of the Master. How could someone so powerful—the Messiah promised by the Father—be taken by human forces? The disciples were listening only superficially, and so Jesus used one of my favorite expressions: "Let these sayings sink down in your ears."

Listening on More than One Level

Your listening skills have a great deal to do with the quality of the relationships you build with others. Think about the number of times you have heard your spouse or parent complain, "You are not hearing what I am saying." In fact, you may have heard the actual words someone spoke, but you did not discern the meaning of the information communicated. A good listener is able to obtain information on several levels and will not only learn more but also understand more. The sad fact is that by nature, we are poor listeners. Studies have shown that we actually retain only 25 to 50 percent of what we hear. That represents a failing grade in listening skills.

It is imperative to become a good listener if we want to avoid being tactless and saying the wrong thing to those to whom we are witnessing. When people believe they are really being heard, they feel you have made them important. They will feel cared for. If someone believes you care about him and are really listening, he will be more likely to return the compliment and hear you out. After all, if you have shown the discernment to recognize the value of his thoughts, why shouldn't he return the same courtesy? Listen closely to make sure you are on the same wavelength and are focused on the same topic.

Why Are We Poor Listeners?

Four independent studies overlap on four major reasons why we are such poor listeners. Commonly, the first reason is a general lack of respect for the speaker. When we do not hold the speaker in high regard, what we hear resembles the cartoon bubble insert, "Blah, blah, blah ..." We know we don't like him, so obviously we won't like what he says. Overcoming prejudice against the speaker requires a conscious effort to separate the individual from the content of his message.

The second most common reason for not listening is obsessive devotion to ourselves. We get so trapped in our personal thoughts and agendas that nothing else gets into the processor. The ears may hear the sounds, but our brains are fully engaged in thinking only about what is of interest to us. Next on the list of reasons for poor listening is related to a resistance to change. Many will listen to words in a superficial way but refuse to allow the depth of the communication to enter in. Keeping the communication on the surface and not entertaining meaning is a safe way to protect our preconceived judgments and opinions. Selective listening allows us to pick and choose what we want to hear. We are poor listeners because we do not want to hear anything contrary to our beliefs. The last common reason cited in studies is a general ignorance about social politeness. "Oh, was I supposed to be listening?" I just find that reason hard to believe.

Learning to Be a Better Listener

If you want to become a better listener, you can. It takes persistence, practice, and the commitment to rise above your selfishness. Improving your listening skills will help you, personally and professionally. Consider certain jobs in which listening is essential. What would you think of a 911 emergency operator who didn't let the report of a car accident with severe injuries process in his brain but just sent a squad car when clearly an ambulance was needed. Just suppose your doctor didn't listen to the serious symptom of chest pain accompanying an inability to raise your left arm and prescribed what she always did for arthritis. These professionals need to be good listeners in order to make correct judgments. Our job is even more critical; to communicate the love and saving power of Jesus Christ. Listening is essential!

Sometimes the best way to move into positive territory is to find the part we play on the negative side of the equation. The following descriptions show some poor listening techniques. See if you can find your own bad habits in one or more these areas,

The pseudo-listener: This is a favorite technique of politicians. Pseudo-listeners are skilled in tuning out the speaker while still giving the appearance of really processing what is being said. They can be very deceptive, knowing just when to nod the head or utter an affirming "uh huh," while never having listened to a word. I had the opportunity of speaking with a former Virginia senator about a controversial issue. It was as if a glaze covered his eyes when I mentioned the subject. What his pseudo-listening conveyed to me was his lack of respect and his lack of interest in something I considered vital. Of course, it is highly unlikely that I would value his candidacy in the future.

Selective listening: This is the more adult version of pseudo-listening. Selective listeners will listen to part of what you are saying, specifically the parts they want to hear. They screen out areas they disagree with or find boring. Christians are very good at this, especially if the pastor preaches a message that touches on their pet sin. Selective listeners will cheer on the exhortation that covers other people's failures but completely ignore the issues of their own sins. Children know how to listen selectively. Tell Johnny you will buy him an ice cream if he cleans his room, and all he will remember is the part about ice cream.

The literal listener: When I was a child, television was still a novelty. Friday nights were a special treat because I got to watch Jack Webb, as Sergeant Joe Friday, fight crime on *Dragnet*. One of Sergeant Friday's often-repeated lines came when he was about to question a witness. If the witness began a protracted answer, Sgt. Friday would say, "Just the facts, ma'am; only the facts." The literal listener follows the Jack Webb model and extracts the hard facts from what he hears. This may be fine when it comes to gleaning information from a college lecture, but it is a poor substitute for true communication.

To really listen, the hearer must be aware of many other factors, such as body language, tone of voice, and context of communication. All these things can impact the message being sent and received. I confess this is a difficulty I have to overcome. A good example of a literal listener is the man who notices his wife is silent and asks, "What's wrong." She replies, "Nothing!" He takes her response literally, although her body language and tone expresses quite the opposite. (He walks away wondering what's for dinner, while she plans an extended vacation in the Bahamas, alone.) Literal listeners are usually shocked when a situation implodes because of their lack of response. After all, she said nothing was wrong, and the husband took her at her word.

Ambush listeners--aka "bushwhackers"

If you have ever watched a political debate, you have seen the ambush listener in action. Everything the speaker says is carefully analyzed for possible ammunition to make the opponent appear in a negative light. The point of the debate is to further your own point of view and negate the points made by the opposition. This is also known as bushwhacking. While bushwhacking is expected behavior in a debate, it is toxic to a relationship. It destroys any possibility of confidentiality and trust. An ambush listener is constantly building an arsenal of information for purposes of attack. If you want to build a relationship where you can share your faith, you will probably not achieve your goal if you engage in this kind of listening. True friends are willing to be vulnerable to one another, but once attacked, most people will not permit further exposure.

I have firsthand experience with this issue because my mom was a bushwhacker. She always encouraged me to share what was going on in my life, and she would listen attentively, but the following week she would use the shared information against me in a barrage of criticism. Obviously, it did not take long for me to learn to respond with one-word answers. Looking at the relationship through the eyes of an adult, I know that my mother's motives were only to improve and instruct her child, but once betrayed and the trust level destroyed, so was the possibility of my receiving any input from her at all. Watch out that your sincere desire to correct doesn't cast you in the roll of a bushwhacker.

"Monopolizers," aka the center of the universe

A person monopolizing a conversation is difficult to consider a listener at all. Actually, this person does listen, but only long enough to find the key to legitimize telling another story from his or her personal repertoire. No matter the subject, the monopolizer will find something to say. The monopolizer will frequently play a game of "can you top this" in an effort to outdo the previous speaker. This person must be the center of attention and the star of the show.

I hesitate to use my mother as an example again, but I must. She excelled at taking over any conversation and making it the opening act for her own performance. A prime example occurred when my grandmother was in a Jewish nursing home in the Bronx. Her roommate. Mrs. Siegel, was a fascinating person who retired from teaching school and moved to Israel to live out her remaining days. Mrs. Siegel was in Israel prior to the Six-Day War of 1967. During this time, guerilla fighters from the Arab Fedayeen executed surprise attacks against both Israeli soldiers and civilians. Mrs. Siegel was injured when the balcony of her apartment was damaged by artillery fire. She fell over the debris and broke a leg during evacuation. Since she lived alone in Israel, her grown children arranged for her to fly back to the United States for medical treatment. This dynamic lady had so many rich stories to tell. I found myself visiting at her bedside nearly as much as with my own grandmother. Of course, my mother was always in the midst of the conversation. It seemed to me that every time Mrs. Siegel started to talk about her experiences in Israel, Mother would cut in and find some remote way to relate the topic to her own life circumstances. I wanted to say, "Shut up, listen, and learn," but she was my mother and that would not have been acceptable. I regret missing several opportunities to get a firsthand viewpoint of an important event in world history because of a monopolizer.

Monopolizers communicate little interest in anyone but themselves. The outflow of conversation far exceeds input from those they hope to reach. If you hope to share your faith and you recognize these tendencies in yourself, remember that Jesus is the star of the show and must be the focus in every relationship.

Becoming an Active Listener

An active listener makes a conscious effort to hear not only the words spoken by another, but the complete message being sent. If you are to succeed, your attention must be carefully fixed on the other person, with the goal of understanding. Active listening is really just an extension of the Golden Rule. How do you want someone to listen to you? Give that same courtesy to others. Right attitude is a major part of active listening.

I tried a little experiment when I was an undergraduate, taking my first class in public speaking. I decided to focus on the speaker and become a positive and proactive listener. When a student assumed the podium, my full attention was on her. I consciously thought of encouragement that I hoped would be communicated. As student after student struggled with insecurity at the lectern, my nonverbal affirmation had impact. After several classes, the professor stopped the flow of presentations and asked why the speakers all found it necessary to focus their attention on Thea. Most did not realize they had directed their presentation to me, but it was apparent to other spectators. Attitude is a key to opening a channel of communication and will cause others to focus on what you have to say when it is your turn to speak.

Some Concrete Tips for Better Listening

1- Avoid distraction: You cannot pay the needed attention to a speaker when you are distracted by a TV, radio, or cell phone. Turn them off! Focus your attention, and do not daydream.

2- Avoid getting bored. Remember the importance of why you are reaching out, so consciously generate ongoing interest.

3- Allow the speaker to finish before you speak. Don't mentally formulate your response while the other person is speaking. The Holy Spirit will give you the words you need when you need them (Matt. 10:19–20).

4- Be aware of gestures and feeling words. Be particularly alert to spot a conflict between what is said and what is communicated. Feeling words can be positive or negative. (Positive words: love, affection, joy, happiness, interest, laughter. Negative words: depression, sadness, distress, fear, anger, anxiety.)

5- From time to time, summarize what you think is being communicated. An example is, "Sounds like you are saying …" or "What I am hearing is …"

6- Ask questions to clarify a point. "What do you mean when you say …?" "Is this what you mean?"

7- Physical proximity: Be close enough to hear clearly and to make eye contact but not so close as to cause discomfort. Get the "feel" for proper distance.

Turning the Conversation to Jesus

Now that you are on your way to open channels of communication, it is important to have a plan to turn the conversation to Jesus. This can be a challenge, but there are some things you can do to smooth awkward moments in conversation. First of all, don't lose sight of the goal of introducing your friend to Jesus Christ. It is very important that you spend time in prayer before the conversation takes place. All of the factors covered in other chapters come into play here. Remember, it is the Father that draws and the Holy Spirit that brings conviction, not you. Be sensitive to the leading of the Holy Spirit, who will guide you at every step. If you meet resistance, perhaps the time is not right. Don't give up; redouble your prayer for that individual.

I Didn't Know He Was Missing

A good way to change the direction of a conversation and turn it toward the Lord is to ask questions. A wise evangelist will be prepared for any answer. Recently, I watched a comedy where one character asked a direct question: "Have you found Jesus?" The response, accompanied by a smirk, was "I didn't know He was missing." The answer confounded the attempt to witness because she was not prepared for a wise-crack response. The subject was immediately dropped. You will not be able to anticipate all responses, but be as prepared with a turnaround as you can be. Your initial question might be just to get the focus on spiritual matters. "Do you ever think about spiritual things?" Follow-up questions might lead to a question about what "spiritual" means. If your friend has confided an experience, you might ask, "How has this experience changed the way you think about God?" Turn-around questions should be relative to your relationship and circumstance. Seek the Holy Spirit to give you leading.

I cannot emphasize enough that you must be sensitive to the response. I remember a time before my father had committed to following Jesus. My cousin, a missionary evangelist on leave from Argentina, wanted to turn the conversation, and so he asked Dad a commonly used question. "If you should die tonight, why would God let you into His heaven?" My father avoided an answer and later expressed to mother and me that he was insulted. Imagine this young man asking him such a question. Dad attended church all his life. Perhaps it was neither the correct question nor the right time. If this response happens to you, don't be concerned. The Lord can use it anyway. God's timing is perfect.

If your conversation successfully turns to Jesus, and it is appropriate for you to share your testimony, always ask permission first. A possible lead in is, "May I share with you my experience in a similar situation?" If the response is negative, you can always open the door to future contact. "Perhaps another time" is a comment not really needing an answer. Don't be discouraged. This is just a signal to you that more prayer is needed for the individual. Always remember, you may be planting or watering a seed that someone else planted. God's timing is perfect.

If you are blessed to be the harvester, here are some points to remember:

a. God's love for the individual
b. The need for a remedy for sin
c. Jesus's death on the cross for our sin
d. His resurrection; the hope we have in following Jesus
e. The need to make an individual commitment to follow Jesus
f. Invite the person to pray with you and commit his or her life to Jesus Christ.

When to Harvest

The right time to harvest is something that must be led by the Holy Spirit. Harvesting too soon can be like picking a tomato when it is still green. If picked too soon, it may never get ripe or develop the full flavor the Lord intended it to have. The wise thing to do is let the tomato ripen on the vine until it is ready to be picked. A spiritual harvest is similar, and so we must be very attentive to the leading of the Spirit. Eager evangelists will rush people into saying a sinner's prayer when there is no real repentance, no actual heart belief. People are quite willing to recite a prayer for their relief and not for their belief. Premature harvesting has been called "sloppy agape" and "greasy grace" because the spiritual experience is only on the surface. There is no questionnaire to be completed by a candidate for salvation, but a Spirit-sensitive harvester will look for certain indicators that the time is right.

1- Is there an awareness of personal sin and the need for a Savior?
2- Does he know who Jesus is (the Word made flesh)?
3- Does he know what Jesus did to pay the penalty for his personal sin?
4- Does he acknowledge that Jesus is the *only* way?
5- Is he ready to place his whole trust and faith in Jesus as payment for his sin and trust in the resurrection to ensure his eternal life?

If the indicators are all yes, by all means pick that tomato and harvest now!

Study/Teaching Outline "Let This Sink Down in Your Ears"

Building Your Confidence-
- Review of what we have studied so far.
  - The Problem of Selfishness—getting out of self
  - The Truth about Consequences—the destiny of the lost
  - God Does All the Heavy Lifting—how people get saved
  - The Dirty Word—why we reach out
  - Yes, You Can!— your personality and styles of evangelism
  - Tell It Like It Is—constructing an effective testimony
  - Let This Sink Down in Your Ears—becoming a good listener

Becoming a Good Listener
- Outreach is the opposite of self-focus. In doing outreach, we get to cooperate with the Lord in three steps:
  - Planting seeds
  - Watering seeds
  - Harvesting
    "I have planted, Apollos watered; but God gave the increase"(1 Cor. 3:6).

- If we are doing our job, we are constantly planting "word" seeds. (It becomes who we are!)
- We are constantly watering by the example of our lifestyle (which must point to Jesus).
- How do we know when the harvest is ripe? "The fields are white to harvest" (John 4:35).

Developing Good Listening Skills

- The importance of listening
  - How well you listen has a major impact on the quality of your relationships.
  - A good listener:
    - obtains more information;
    - understands and learns more.
- We are, by nature, poor listeners. Studies show we remember only between 25 and 50% of what we hear.
- Reasons to improve listening skills for sharing your faith
  - To avoid saying the wrong thing; being tactless.
  - To generate a genuine feeling of caring.
  - To help people want to start listening to you.
  - To increase the other person's confidence in you.
  - To make the other person feel important and recognized.
  - To be sure you both are on the same wavelength.
  - To be sure you both are focused on the same topic.
- Why do we have such poor listening skills? (Four independent studies overlap key reasons.)
  - Lack of respect for the speaker. (We really don't care about the other guy.)
  - Stuck in own head; trapped by own thoughts. (Thinking about our own agenda.)
  - Hearing only what is superficially said; missing the real meaning.
  - General ignorance about social politeness.
- Listening is a skill that may be learned and practiced.
  - Improving listening skills takes practice, but it can be done.
  - Requires persistence and deliberate attention to the task at hand.

- For some jobs, listening actively and taking in what is said is critical (e.g., 911 operator).
- Improving your listening skills helps you both professionally and personally.
- Our job is to communicate the love and saving power of Jesus Christ. Listening is essential.

Types of poor listening skills (Find your personal bad habits.)
- Pseudo-listening—"tuning out" the speaker
  - Pseudo-listening gives the appearance of attentiveness without really processing what the speaker is saying.
  - Pseudo-listeners can fool you. They pick up on appropriate moments to nod or say "uh huh" so that the speaker believes they are listening when they are not.
    - (Common example: a child, when a parent or teacher lectures on appropriate behavior. The child tunes out, and the substance of the talk is lost.)
- Selective listening (the more adult version of pseudo-listening)
  - Selective listeners only listen to the parts of the message that they want to hear.
  - Screens out information they find boring or things with which they disagree
    - (example: tuning out the parts of pastor's message that deals with your pet sin).
- Literal listening (just the facts, please)
  - Only paying attention to the literal content of a message.
  - Ignoring other factors such as tone of voice, body language, and context that may influence meaning (example: you ask your wife what is wrong, and she says nothing! You take her response literally and walk away, although her expression says something is definitely amiss).
- Ambush listeners (targeting the speaker)
  - "Ambushing" is listening for the purpose of finding something that can be used against a person.
  - Common example is a political debate. A candidate listens to an opponent for the purpose of using his words against him.

- ○ Ambushing is particularly damaging to relationships because it destroys trust.
  - ○ Ambushers fail to consider the speaker's perspective.
  - ○ It can be hard to have an open, honest conversation with an ambush listener.
- Monopolizers (those who think they are the "center of the universe")
  - ○ Monopolizers listen for an opportunity to refocus the conversation on themselves. (Example: speaker says, "My husband is always working late." You reply, "That's nothing. My husband …" and you proceed to tell her about your husband's late hours.)
  - ○ Monopolizers focus is on *self* and communicate little interest in the speaker or the speaker's problems.

Taking steps to improve listening skills.
- Become an active listener.
  - ○ Active listening is where you make a conscious effort to hear not only the words that another person is saying but the complete message being sent.
  - ○ (Remember, our job is to communicate the love of Jesus and His power to save.)
    - ▪ To do this, you must pay attention to the other person very carefully.
  - ○ Active listening is really an extension of the Golden Rule. (To know how to listen to someone else, think about how you would want someone to listen to you.)
- Beware of distractions.
  - ○ You cannot allow yourself to become distracted by what is around you (turn off TV, cell phone, etc.).
  - ○ Don't formulate a counter-argument to use when the other person stops speaking.
  - ○ Do not permit boredom to cause you to lose focus on what the other person is saying. Generate interest. Remember the importance of why you are reaching out.

- All of the above reasons contribute to a lack of listening and understanding.
  - Old habits are hard to break. It takes concentration and determination to be an active listener
  - Be deliberate in listening and remind yourself frequently that your goal is to truly hear what the other person is saying.
  - Set aside all other thoughts and behaviors and concentrate on the message
- Some concrete tips for active listening
  - Be physically close enough to the person you are listening to so you can hear clearly.
  - Turn off any background noise such as a radio, TV, or cell phone.
  - Concentrate on what is being said. Do not daydream; stay focused on the person.
  - Be aware of gestures. This includes facial expressions, body language, and tone.
  - Eye contact: direct your eyes to the person talking to you.
  - Ask questions to verify everything that you do not understand.
  - Acknowledgement: give occasional nonverbal feedback. Nod your head and use appropriate facial expressions.
  - Allow the speaker to finish before you speak. (You can not actively listen if you are thinking about what you are going to ask.)
  - Listen for "feeling words." Try to identify the person's feeling and then reflect them back to the speaker.
    - Positive feeling words: love, affection, concern, interest, elation, and joy.
    - Negative feeling words: depression, sadness, distress, fear, anger, and anxiety.
  - Reflect what has been said by paraphrasing. Example: "What I'm hearing is …" and "Sounds like you are saying …"
  - Ask questions to clarify certain points. "What do you mean when you say …" or "Is this what you mean?"

- ○ Summarize the speaker's comments periodically.
  - ▪ People are more open if they know you understand them. "This you know, my beloved brethren. But everyone must be quick to hear, slow to speak and slow to anger" (James 1:19).

Turning the Conversation to Point to Jesus
- Purpose is always to point to Jesus. *This is essential*!
- Be careful that *you* do not become the hero of the situation.
- Point to Jesus and not yourself. (Do not even point to the church.)
- Listen for the leading of the Holy Spirit in how to turn around the conversation.

Harvest time is now
- The harvest is out there waiting for you: "Therefore said He unto them, The harvest truly [is] great, but the laborers [are] few: pray ye therefore the Lord of the harvest, that He would send forth laborers into His harvest" (Luke 10:2).
- The harvest is ready now! "Say not ye, There are yet four months, and [then] cometh harvest? Behold, I say unto you, Lift up your eyes, and look on the fields; for they are white already to harvest" (John 4:35).
- Now is the day of salvation: "For He saith, I have heard thee in a time accepted and in the day of salvation have I succored thee; behold, now [is] the accepted time; behold, now [is] the day of salvation" (2 Cor. 6:2).
- There is coming a time when it will be too late! "Let both grow together until the harvest; and in the time of the harvest I will say to the reapers, Gather ye together first the tares and bind them in bundles to burn them: but gather the wheat into my barn" (Matt. 13:30).
- Harvest now! "Behold, He cometh with clouds; and every eye shall see Him, and they [also] which pierced Him: and all kindreds of the earth shall wail because of Him" (Rev. 1:7).
  - ○ Harvest now because you don't know when that day will be: "For yourselves know perfectly that the day of the Lord so cometh as a thief in the night" (1 Thess. 5:2).

- ○ "I must work the works of him that sent me, while it is day: the night cometh, when no man can work" (John 9:4).
- ○ Suddenly, time's up: "Watch therefore: for ye know not what hour your Lord doth come" (Matt. 24:42–44). "Therefore be ye also ready: for in such an hour as ye think not the Son of man cometh" (Matt. 24:44–51).
- The doors are still open today. "And the Spirit and the bride say, Come. And let him that heareth say, Come. And let him that is athirst come. And whosoever will, let him take the water of life freely" (Rev. 22:17–20).

"Turn the Beat Around"

Practice Scenarios

(The following scenarios are used by permission of Kelly Diehl, a dedicated teacher and youth minister at Kingdom Life Ministries in Chesapeake, Virginia.)

How would you turn the following conversations to include the Lord Jesus Christ?

1. You have met a seventeen-year-old guy from California who just moved to the area. You ask him why he didn't believe in God, and he said there was a certain way that he wanted to live his life and that God and Jesus and all of that got in the way. He told you that to believe in God and Jesus takes a full commitment. He said it is something you should do with all that you are, and that he couldn't do that. He was even able to quote Scripture, where Jesus talked about counting the cost before you join. He said he just wasn't ready, but maybe he would be someday. He had "things to do" before he could give up his life. How do you respond?

2. You are talking with the mother of one of your kid's playmates. She seems sad and mentions that she and her husband are splitting up. They are Roman Catholic, and she will not be able to take Communion in her church. What do you say to or offer her?

3. Your friend just told you that her boyfriend asked her to have sex with her, and she doesn't know what to do. She loves him, but if her parents find out she knows they will "kill" her. How do you respond and enter into talking about God?

4. You are eating lunch with a coworker who is single. She is struggling because she really wants a husband and has given up. She is very discouraged. How do you encourage her and bring Christ into the situation?

5. You see a Facebook post from a friend that reads, "I don't believe in God. If He was real, he would never have let my best friend die." How do you respond?

6. You are at the grocery store in line and overhear a mother and daughter arguing. You turn around and smile, and the mother apologizes to you. How do you respond, and how can you lead into a conversation about God?

7. You meet up with a friend who is really depressed. She is taking care of an older parent and hasn't been able to go out much and is drained. How can you encourage her and enter into a conversation about a relationship with God?

8. Your coworker has been stressed out at work and hasn't been herself. She shared that she hasn't been sleeping at night because she is worried about her husband leaving her. She confided in you about some things she has seen on her husband's computer. How do you respond?

9. Your neighbor's father just passed away. He says he is mad at God, and He should not have allowed this to happen. How do you respond?

10. Your older child is a backslider. You keep telling him he needs to get back in church. He knows the way, but is just living a life of rebellion. He comes home for Christmas to visit and tells you

he is a relationship with the same sex. How do you respond, staying true to Scripture and still sharing the love of Jesus?

11. You are at the grocery store and begin small talk with the grocery clerk. You see a cross necklace around his neck and begin talking about church. He mentions he has been hurt by church and doesn't trust people anymore. What can you say to him?

12. Your best friend has just found out he has cancer. The doctors did not give him a good report, and he is very depressed and just wants to die now. You know that his relationship with God has not been consistent. How do you witness to him?

13. You find a woman crying on a park bench. You ask her if everything is okay, and she proceeds to tell you that she is trying to escape a life of prostitution and heroin addiction. You tell her about the forgiveness of God, but she says, "I am way too far gone for God's forgiveness. You have no idea what I've done." How do you respond?

14. You are in line at Starbucks, waiting on a venti vanilla latte. The person in line behind you asks if you know whether or not there is a Home Depot in town. You get the feeling he is new to town. Engage him in a conversation and turn the focus toward the Lord.

15. You are pulling weeds, and your next-door neighbor comes by. You two chit-chat, and you mention that you are eager to get the weeds pulled today because you'll be involved in church activities most of the next day. He says, "I don't understand what you get out of that church stuff anyway! No one has all the answers or proof of anything, and all the different religions seem to do is fight and scrap with each other. Don't you think it's a waste of time?" How would you respond?

16. You have an older brother who lives across the country, so you rarely see him. You know from his statements and actions that he is not a Christian. He has lived an interesting life, but now is a stable businessman, husband, and father. You witnessed to him many years ago as a new believer. You were pretty pushy, and he rejected all of it. He has come to visit for the Christmas holiday, and you are at the dinner table, talking about life and updating each other on how things have been. How do you engage in a conversation about God?

17. You run into a neighbor and ask her how her day was. Not so good—she lost her purse, damaged her car, and her refrigerator broke. It was an hour after you had said good-bye that you realized you should have prayed for her and offered to help. You kicked yourself for missing the opportunity but then realized you really hadn't. You go to her house and knock on her door. What do you say?

CHAPTER EIGHT

Your Honor, I Object!

(Common Objections)

There will always be those who object to the good news message of salvation through the blood of Jesus Christ. Objections can be sincere or pretended. A sincere objection carries with it the desire to learn the answer to a question, while the intent of the pretended objection is to deflect the conversation away from a sensitive area. One teacher suggests asking the following question to determine the sincerity of the objection: "If I answer your question, will it make a difference to your life?" This may seem rather strong, but it is important that you are not taken off course. When Jesus conversed with the Samaritan woman, she tried to change the subject from her own past to a controversial religious question. Jesus would not allow her to do it (John 4:19–20). Answering her question would not have made a big difference in her life, but offering her living water changed her eternity.

You do not have to be a theologian to be an effective witness, but it is important to be aware of what you believe and have a ready answer to bring truth to the truth-seeker. Begin by exercising your listening skills and restate what you think the objection really is. Think about a Scripture reference that would lead to the answer. If you do not know the answer, acknowledge it. Offering to find more information and get back to the questioner is an acceptable response. If you find that the objection raised is not sincere or is followed by a barrage of additional questions, do not hesitate to defer answering to a later time, or redirect the questioner to a more experienced Christian. Whether or not the question is genuine, it is important to check the tone of your response. Be careful not to get angry or appear haughty. Stay humble and stay tuned in to the Holy Spirit's leading. Remember, those with no relationship with Jesus Christ are in the dark spiritually. Sometimes poking a little hole in someone's objection will allow the light of the Word to do its work.

What Questions Can I Expect?

The following questions were suggested by a forum of pastors as the most common objections, in their collective experiences. The answers given are far from complete but only serve to change the direction of the conversation and point to Jesus. If you have a particular interest in any of these areas, I encourage you to study and become an expert. For most of us, however, our job is not to give a doctoral dissertation on any topic but to point the way to the *only way*!

Determining the real objection means listening. The question as verbalized may not be the real issue at all, and it takes listening skill to find the question behind the question. If the questioner is more than a casual contact, try to determine what is motivating the inquiry. This may open a more effective opportunity to share the gospel. Above all, be sensitive.

Objection #1—"I don't believe in God. I am an atheist [or agnostic]."

The atheist sees himself as too smart to believe in "fables" about God. He believes he has scientifically dispensed with ancient superstitious explanations for natural phenomena. Actually, the atheist is very religious, but his faith is in science. A major problem of faith in science is the frequency of change in the content of what is dogmatically taught. What scientists believe to be true in one era becomes the superstition of the next generation. There is a minimal difference between the atheist and the agnostic. Atheists say that God does not exist, while the agnostic says maybe God exists but we can't know anything about Him. Both views have a fatal flaw. Saying there is no God with any surety requires the individual to know everything about everything. Since this is impossible, a dogmatic exclusion of the existence of God is also not possible. An agnostic says, "There is one thing I know about God—that we cannot know anything about God." If you are saying "huh?" remember what the Bible says about these folks:

"The fool hath said in his heart, There is no God. They are corrupt, they have done abominable works, there is none that doeth good" (Ps. 14:1; 53:1).

Digging a little deeper, there is often a secondary motivation behind both these worldviews. If there is no God, then there is no right or wrong and therefore, no such thing as sin. If there is no God, then I am not accountable to anyone other than myself, and I am free to do precisely as I choose. Be aware of this possibility in witnessing to a proclaimed atheist or agnostic. No matter the motivation, it is essential to pray that they be given the gift of understanding and faith in Jesus Christ. They are not our enemies; the god of this world who has blinded them is our real foe (2 Cor. 4:4).

Poking Little Light Holes into the "No-God" Darkness

Many evangelists have addressed this objection using the concept of "original cause." After current scientific understanding takes its best shot at explaining phenomena, there is always a question of a first, original, and primary cause for everything. Both the Bible and science acknowledge that the universe had a beginning and that it could not have come into existence without a force behind it. This is a good starting place because there is agreement. Every effect has a cause behind it. Here are some areas you might want to reference in affirming a very basic belief in the existence of God.

1- Every creation has a creator. The Bible points toward the Creator, revealing His glory. "The heavens declare the glory of God; and the firmament sheweth his handywork. Day unto day uttereth speech, and night unto night sheweth knowledge. There is no speech nor language, where their voice is not heard" (Ps. 19:1–3).

2- Every design has a designer. Everything surrounding us has an intricate design, from the vastness of the universe to the unique strands of DNA in every cell of our bodies. These do not randomly occur but testify to the greatness of God. His design is maintained by the work of Jesus Christ.

3- "For by him were all things created, that are in heaven, and that are in earth, visible and invisible, whether they be thrones, or dominions, or principalities, or powers: all things were created by him, and for him: And he is before all things, and by him all things consist" (Col. 1:16–17).

4- Every law has a lawgiver. A sense of moral right and wrong is universal, transcends cultures, and comes from an outside source. What we call a "conscience" comes from God Himself. "For when the Gentiles, which have not the law, do by nature the things contained in the law, these, having not the law, are a law unto themselves: Which shew the work of the law written in their hearts, their conscience also bearing witness, and their thoughts the mean while accusing or else excusing one another" (Romans 2:14–15).

Turning the Conversation to Jesus

We are made in the image of God, intricately designed to be in fellowship with our Creator. God created us with a conscience that tells us we are not in right standing with Him. Nobody in the world has been able to keep God's moral code perfectly, except Jesus Christ. This reveals that all humans need forgiveness and are in desperate need of a Savior. We can deny the voice of our consciences, but ultimately we will have to make a decision concerning Jesus. In the end, every knee shall bow to Him, and every voice will proclaim that He is Lord to the glory of God the Father.

> Wherefore God also hath highly exalted him, and given him a name which is above every name: That at the name of Jesus every knee should bow, of things in heaven, and things in mud, and things under the earth;

And that every tongue should confess that Jesus Christ
is Lord, to the glory of God the Father. (Phil. 2:9–11)

The Word of God clearly states that God wants to be known. We
are created with a will, emotions, and the intellect to appreciate the one
who made us (Jer. 29:13; Prov. 8:17; Zeph. 2:3). Jesus was incarnate
in human form but never ceased to be the express image of the Father.
We can know the Father through His only begotten Son, Jesus Christ
(Heb. 1:1–3).

Objection #2—"What about evolution? Doesn't that contradict creation?"

Several generations, including my own, have been taught that
evolution was a fact when it is (and always has been) only a theory.
Scientific finds of the last fifty years have cast serious doubts that Mr.
Darwin's theory was right; yet to my knowledge his ideas about the
origins of species are still taught in American public schools. Why is
this, and why are the evidences for divine creation ignored? Simply put,
Darwinism was the key that liberated mankind from accountability to
a Creator. Those rejecting biblical truth do not want to lose that key.
Furthermore, educators, driven by multicultural political correctness do
not want to teach anything that would authenticate the Judeo-Christian
position. If the schools taught all views, they would not have time
to teach anything else, and so the truth of creation is ignored simply
because it is God's truth. Christians are portrayed as ignorant people,
blinded by charismatic leaders. It is just too much for the intelligentsia
of the educational community to admit the Bible has been right all
along. Paul said this about those of us who are called to be Christians:

For ye see your calling, brethren, how that not many
wise men after the flesh, not many mighty, not many
noble, are called: But God hath chosen the foolish
things of the world to confound the wise; and God
hath chosen the weak things of the world to confound

the things which are mighty; And base things of the world, and things which are despised, hath God chosen, yea, and things which are not, to bring to nought things that are: That no flesh should glory in his presence. (1 Cor. 1:26–29)

For those of us who know we are "nots," we are happy to cling to our Bibles and the truths in it. Our task here is not to present a scholarly work on what is wrong with the theory of evolution but to humbly present some of the contradictions, supported by science. Our goal is to poke a little light hole in the black box of evolution that will open the door to the truth of the Word of God.

Pinpoints of Light

A young earth: In order for the theory of evolution to function, the earth would have to be capable of supporting life for millions of years. Here is a quote from a secular scientist concerning the viability of an "old earth" theory. He zeroes in on the strength of the magnetic field necessary for life.

> Dr. Thomas Barnes, Emeritus Professor of Physics at the University of Texas at El Paso, published the definitive work in this field. Scientific observations since 1829 have shown that the earth's magnetic field has been measurably decaying at an exponential rate, demonstrating its half-life to be approximately 1,400 years. In practical application its strength 20,000 years ago would approximate that of a magnetic star. Under those conditions many of the atoms necessary for life processes could not form. This data demonstrate that earth's entire history is young, within a few thousand of years. (Thomas Barnes, ICR Technical Monograph #4, *Origin and Destiny of the Earth's Magnetic Field*, 1983)

The environment on or near a magnetic star would preclude the formation or survival of life. The presence of a magnetic star would cause the atoms that form our bodies, trees, animals, water, and earth to be unable to adhere to each other. This one basic fact confirms all of evolutionary theory to be bad science, at best."

The fossil record: If Darwin's theory of evolution were factual, there would be fossil evidence to support the altering of one species into another. There would be an abundance of intermediary forms in the strata of the earth. The earth's surface is deposited in layers, and animals appear suddenly in what is called the Cambrian Period. Only a few multicellular fossils appear in earlier layers. The animal fossils in the Cambrian layer are fully developed an not in some state of gradual formation. Some creatures appear in multiple layers. Here are two quotes from secular scientists commenting on "polystrata fossils" and the lack of transitional forms (missing links):

> This supposed column is actually saturated with 'polystrata fossils' (fossils extending from one geologic layer to another) that tie all the layers to one time-frame. To the unprejudiced, the fossil record of plants is in favor of special creation.[3]

Transitional forms:

> "The lack of transitional series cannot be explained as being due to the scarcity of material. The deficiencies are real, they will never be filled" (N. Heribert Nilsson, as quoted in Arthur C. Custance, *The Earth Before Man, Part II,* Doorway Papers, no. 20. Ontario, Canada: Doorway Publications, p. 51).

God's special creation is the only viable explanation for the origin of life and biological design. Remember, these are only pinpoints of light to be presented prayerfully to open your seeker to the truth of

---

[3] (E. J. H. Corner, *Contemporary Botanical Thought,* ed. A. M. MacLeod and L. S. Cobley. Chicago: Quadrangle Books, 1961, p. 97)

God's Word. Keep your responses simple and humble. Acknowledge that species have physically adapted over time in order to survive but did not form entirely new species. Claims that new species came from these adaptations are just not supported by fact.

There are some other theories with which you should be familiar. The first is that life evolved randomly from nonliving material. The mathematical probability that life popped into existence at random is so miniscule that the concept is considered by many scientists to be absurd. Another bizarre thought is that all life originated as a kind of "chemical ooze." Current research in molecular biology has revealed the complex structure of proteins, nucleic acids, and amino acids in DNA. The idea that life could have spontaneously arisen in the same place at the same time by chance takes much more faith to believe than the special creation account of the book of Genesis. It is irrational to think that something spontaneously came from nothing or that order suddenly appeared out of chaos and that consciousness came from primitive chowder.

Remember that those who believe in these theories view the beliefs of creationists as equally preposterous. We are not in the business of insulting others but only want to open the window to God's truth.

Objection #3—"How do I know the Bible is true? What about errors and contradictions? The Bible is full of errors."

This is one of my favorite objections because the next logical step is asking the objector another question: "Have you ever read the Bible?" You'd be surprised at the number of people who glibly raise this objection but have never opened the cover of the Word of God. Their objection is based on hearsay. They once heard someone say that the Bible is full of errors, and that was excuse enough for them not to believe Bible teaching. If objectors say they have read part of the Bible, ask what contradiction or error they found. Most will not have an answer for you. This is often enough to cast some doubt on this secondhand objection. (It may even stimulate them to actually read the Bible.)

What about actual apparent errors or contradictions? What most people claim as errors aren't errors in the Bible at all but a difficulty in translation or in understanding the culture of the time of writing. Sometimes the reader makes an assumption that two similar accounts describe the identical event, when a closer examination of the details shows the events to be different. Most people have not taken the time to search out these possibilities or to do an in-depth study of the passage in question. They take a quick and easy out and chalk up the apparent difficulty to error. Many former difficulties have been resolved by new discoveries in language, archeology, and other sciences. In the original language, the Bible is free from any error. This is called "inerrancy." Within the pages of God's Word, the Bible describes itself as "the word of truth" (2 Cor. 6:7; Col. 1:5; 2 Tim. 2:15; James 1:18). Inerrancy is not a theory about the Bible. It is the teaching of the Bible itself.

A question related to this common objection is, "Why are there so many different versions?" Since the original language of the Old Testament is Hebrew and that of the New Testament is Greek (and some Aramaic), it is not commonly readable to nonscholars. Translation can be difficult, as there isn't always a way to express the same concept across languages. English-speaking people have had the advantage of many translations, some good and some questionable. In a good translation, the meaning of every word can be validated against the original. Within the last fifty years, there also have been several "nontranslations" of the Bible produced for English-speaking people, which attempt to modernize the language by expressing concepts rather than translating words. Although they may be easier to read, these cannot be considered the inerrant Word of God. It is very important that you understand what it is you are reading and studying. To do this, check the publisher's notes to see if it is a translation or a paraphrase or something else. Remember, the further you get away from the original language, the less you can rely on its accuracy.

If you come across a difficulty in the Bible, there are many good books that have delved deeply into troublesome texts. One I have used is *Encyclopedia of Bible Difficulties* (G. Archer, 1982).

Objection #4—"Why is there evil in the world if God is good? What about suffering?"

The real question behind this objection may not be a question at all but a deep-seated hurt. Use your listening skills and be sensitive to what is really being said. Look for areas to minister to the hurt as well as answering the question of evil.

How can the presence of God be consistent with the presence of evil? The short answer is, God created everything to be good (Gen.1:25, 31). Evil is not a creation of God, but He does permit it to exist. Evil is the product of sin, which came into existence when one-third of the angels of heaven believed Lucifer and rebelled against God. Translating evil into the earthly realm followed the same path as it did with fallen angels. Lucifer won the allegiance of God's highest creation when Adam chose to violate the only prohibition God gave him. Adam rebelled against the lordship of his Creator. Evil is the result of sin, and sin entered the world through man's disobedience (Gen. 3).

Why did God permit the existence of an opportunity to sin? The answer is free will. Without the presence of an opportunity to choose between good and evil, both mankind and angelic beings would serve God as robots and not by their choice. The good news is that God provided the solution for evil. He sent His Son, Jesus, to accomplish the ultimate defeat of evil on the cross. All suffering is traceable to the existence of sin. If Adam had not sinned, there would be no suffering and no death (1 Cor. 15:22).

At the heart of this objection is the charge that God is not fair. Innocent children suffer and die, and surely they do not deserve it. Sin produces suffering, and the wages of sin is death. It is a condition that exists on this earth, and the innocent suffer along with the guilty. The epitome of innocent suffering is Jesus Christ Himself. He took what we deserved and paid the price for each one of us. Consider the picture of His suffering.

"He is despised and rejected of men; a man of sorrows, and acquainted with grief: and we hid as it were our faces from him; he was despised, and we esteemed him not. Surely he hath borne our griefs, and carried our sorrows: yet we did esteem him stricken, smitten of

God, and afflicted. But he was wounded for our transgressions, he was bruised for our iniquities: the chastisement of our peace was upon him; and with his stripes we are healed" (Isaiah 53:3–5).

We do not get what we deserve. This is God's mercy. The mercy of God and the price paid by Jesus Christ is explained in 2 Corinthians 5:21 and John 10:10.

"For he hath made him to be sin for us, who knew no sin; that we might be made the righteousness of God in him" (2 Cor. 5:21).

"The thief cometh not, but for to steal, and to kill, and to destroy: I am come that they might have life, and that they might have [it] more abundantly" (John 10:10).

Just as we are waiting for the return of Jesus and the resurrection of the dead, so evil has not yet been removed from the world. What a glorious day that will be!

> But now is Christ risen from the dead, and become the firstfruits of them that slept. For since by man came death, by man came also the resurrection of the dead. For as in Adam all die, even so in Christ shall all be made alive.
>
> But every man in his own order: Christ the firstfruits; afterward they that are Christ's at his coming. Then cometh the end, when he shall have delivered up the kingdom to God, even the Father; when he shall have put down all rule and all authority and power. For he must reign, till he hath put all enemies under his feet. The last enemy that shall be destroyed is death. (1 Cor. 15:20–26)

In addressing the objection of evil, there is a Scripture you need to know. The following quote appears to contradict the fact that God did not create evil:

"I form the light, and create darkness: I make peace, and create evil: I the LORD do all these things" (Isa. 45:7).

If evil is really inconsistent with the work of God, what is this verse saying? First, we need to look at other possible translations for the Hebrew word translated as "evil" in the King James Version. Other major English versions translate the same word as adversity, calamity, distress, and affliction. Because the Hebrew word can refer to moral evil, in order to get the correct perspective, it is important to consider the context. The context of the chapter repeats a common theme—that God rewards Israel for obeying and judges Israel for disobeying. He blesses and saves those He favors and brings disaster on those who rebel against Him. The context supports the idea that the calamity brought by God is in the area of judgment and not that He is the source of moral evil.

Objection #5—"Is hell for real? Why would a loving God send people to hell?"

The question of hell is related to the suffering question in that it also attempts to paint God as unfair. While evil and suffering are very real, they are also very temporary. When God finally deals with evil, He will address all evil, but in the meantime the door to salvation is still open, and atonement for sin is still available through the sacrifice of Jesus. Spending eternity in the presence of the Lord is possible, yet many make the choice not to do it God's way. When there is a refusal to accept Jesus as "the Way," a choice is made. Sadly, the end result of that choice is separation from God, forever and ever. Hell is a choice. God doesn't send anyone there; rather, that choice is made by the individual. Some do not fear hell because they think it is one big immoral party with their friends. Nothing could be further from the truth. Earlier, we examined the descriptions of hell given by Jesus, and so there is no need to repeat the details. A famous atheist had this to say about making the choice for hell: "For God to force people to go to heaven against their wishes wouldn't be heaven—it would be hell. The gates of hell are locked from the inside by the free choice of men and women" (Jean-Paul Sartre, atheist author).

Objection #6—"What about the people who never heard the gospel? Do they go to hell?"

This objection has a dual purpose. First, it is another attempt to demonstrate that God is unfair, but most of all, it serves as a redirect and gets the heat off the one making the objection. When the Holy Spirit is at work convicting an individual of sin, it is very uncomfortable. Just as we want to keep the conversation focused on Jesus, your questioner wants to get the focus off himself and onto someone—anyone—else. Don't let him off the hook! Answer the question and then come back to him with "What about you?"

Romans 2:11–16 speaks about judgment according to the light given in the heart and the testimony of nature. The knowledge of right and wrong is programmed into the heart of man. We call it conscience. Nature also proclaims the glory and majesty of God. The Lord knows how to reveal Himself and will go to extraordinary measures to do so. Consider how Philip was sent the Ethiopian eunuch to explain the very passage he was reading, which "coincidently" spoke of Messiah Jesus. In Matthew 7:7–8, Jesus promises that all who seek Him will find Him. Our Father knows how to keep a divine appointment. There have been many recent testimonies from people who never heard the gospel because they live in Islamic countries but have experienced dreams and visions that led them to faith in Jesus Christ.

Abraham made a statement concerning God that will help you reverse the deflection and return the conversation to the individual and his need for a Savior. Abraham said, "Shall not the judge of all the earth do right?"(Gen. 18:25). Remind the questioner that he has no excuse. The gospel is available to him in many forms, and so he will be held accountable by God for the light he has been given or has the opportunity to acquire. Keep the heat on! Your job is to point him to Jesus, not make him comfortable.

Objection #7—"All religions are the same. Aren't there many ways to get to heaven? Don't all paths ultimately lead to the same place? We all worship the same God, as long as we are sincere."

All religions are not the same, but many share the same standards of right and wrong. In our culture, we call these ethics "Judeo-Christian values." However, ethics are not the same as faith, especially saving faith in Jesus Christ. Ethics are moral standards. Ethics will never save us, because no one except for Jesus ever lived a completely ethical life. Any infraction of the Law makes us guilty of violating the entire Law (James 2:10) and so, left to ourselves, we are in a fatal predicament. The Old Testament outlined an elaborate system of animal sacrifices which foreshadowed the sacrifice of Jesus Christ. The shedding of the blood of these innocent substitutes temporarily covered the sin of Israel, until the permanent price for sin was paid

"But if we walk in the light, as he is in the light, we have fellowship one with another, and the blood of Jesus Christ his Son cleanseth us from all sin" (1 John 1:7).

Unlike other religions, Christianity's founder lives! The grave was not His swan song upon the earth. This is unique to Christianity. Other religions point to a founder whose end was the grave and who will ultimately bow the knee to Jesus as Lord of all. Other paths—other religions and philosophies—are literally dead ends. Jesus clearly said He was the *only* way to the Father (John 14:6). That excludes any other. and so all religions are definitely not the same.

Now let's address the sincerity issue. If a surgeon ignored test results that indicated a ruptured appendix and decided to remove your kidney instead, would his sincere belief that the kidney was the culprit excuse the error? Not likely. When the appendix ruptures, it is the appendix that needs to be removed. Anything else will result in failure. How long have you been doing your best but meeting with failure and falling into sin? Your best is not good enough to please God, because His standard is perfection. If personal best was good enough, then surely the Father would have let Jesus off the hook when He prayed, "Father if it be possible let this cup pass from me" (Matt. 29:36). Your best will never give you eternal life, but God's best is available to you.

Another question closely related to the sincere path is just doing what you feel is right. The doctrine of "right feeling" will put some grease on the path to hell and make your footing even more slippery. Think about the views that others consider right. Islamic terrorists think it is right to destroy innocent lives in order to create fear and chaos. Throughout history, people have been murdered because they did not believe in the same things as a particular group in power. Hitler thought it was right to kill Jews and Gypsies. He was wrong! The Bible states that the heart is deceitful above all things (Jer. 17:9). Feeling right about stealing, lying, killing, and cheating does not make it right. What does the Word of God say? Truth will not contradict itself. Don't allow the dictates of your heart to determine your eternal future.

Objection #8—"Christians are all hypocrites. Why would I want to be one? The Christians I know aren't much different from anyone else."

Be aware that this objection may mask deep-seated hurts suffered at the hands of the church or at the hands of supposed Christians. Handle this objection with extreme gentleness.

The definition of a hypocrite is simple to understand, but it is not always easy to spot one. A hypocrite is an actor, someone pretending to be something he is not. The more skilled the actor, the more you believe the roll he is portraying. Jesus had no difficulty separating the role-player from the true believer and did not soften His words in dealing with the offender.

"Woe unto you, scribes and Pharisees hypocrites! for ye are like unto whited sepulchres, which indeed appear beautiful outwardly, but are within full of dead men's bones, and of all uncleanness. Even so ye also outwardly appear righteous unto men, but within ye are full of hypocrisy and iniquity" (Matt. 23:27–28).

I think Jesus was so harsh with hypocrites because of the extreme harm they do to the lives of others. The apostle Paul warned Titus and young pastor Timothy not to raise untried and unexamined people to positions of leadership. Jesus painted a picture to represent the impact of the damage that can be done through the actions of someone whose life does not reflect the Christian words he teaches. He called them whitewashed sepulchers, looking good from the outside but the inner parts contained only death. A hypocritical leader's impact can have eternal consequences. I have attempted to talk with several young people disillusioned by hypocritical leaders who now reject everything connected with the Lord, including the most basic conversation. To their way of thinking, the fallen leader represented Jesus. Unfortunately, experiences of this nature can become a convenient excuse not to confront personal sinfulness and need for the Savior.

In reality, the church has always had hypocrites in both pew and pulpit. Remember that Jesus never invited us to follow others but to follow Him alone. Gently encourage those who pose this objection to Christianity not to allow the bad behavior of a few rob them of their opportunity for eternal life. We are ultimately individually responsible for our decisions, and pointing to the hypocrisy of another is not a valid excuse for failing to accept the marvelous gift the Father has given to us in the person of His Son, Jesus Christ. The question isn't whether there are hypocrites in the church but whether Jesus is a hypocrite. The Bible testifies that Jesus was perfect and without sin of any kind (2 Cor. 5:21; 1 Peter 2:22; 1 John 3:5; John 8:46). Focusing on evil works committed by hypocrites is a smokescreen to avoid the real issue of personal sin.

Objection #9—"I don't think I am a sinner."

The question of personal sin is probably the most important objection because if we do not recognize that we are sinners, there can be no repentance and no salvation. Most people who deny they are sinners do not know what sin is. God established the standards we are to live by when He gave the Law to the prophet Moses. Sin is falling short of God's standards, as expressed in His commandments. These standards were given to Israel but are not for Israel only. They are for all of us. Now before you go off on the fact that Jesus fulfilled the Law and gave us new commandments (this, of course, is absolutely true), take a look at Paul's description of the Law and how it exposes sin. "Therefore the law was our tutor to bring us to Christ, that we might be justified by faith" (Gal. 3:24 NIV).

"Now we know that whatever the law says, it says to those who are under the law, so that every mouth may be silenced and the whole world held accountable to God. Therefore no one will be declared righteous in God's sight by the works of the law; rather, through the law we become conscious of our sin" (Rom. 3:19–20 NIV).

Paul goes on to instruct us that even he would not have known what sin was without the Law to raise consciousness of what is right and what is not (Rom. 7:7). You can view one of the best practical applications of using the Law to expose sin in a video titled: *Hell's Best Kept Secret* by Ray Comfort and Kirk Cameron. Kirk Cameron is an American actor who has starred in many Christian films, and Ray Comfort is a Christian evangelist who has produced excellent books and videos on practical evangelism. His organization is called the Way of the Master and is located in Bellflower, California. The dialogue Ray uses shows both great skill and sensitivity in using the Ten Commandments to expose sin. He uses a series of questions to get the objector to admit sin without condemnation and then completes the conversation with the plan of salvation. You can view these videos and other excellent material on his website, LivingWaters.com.

Objection #10—"I do many good works. Compared to others, I'm a saint!"

Like many others, before I was a Christian I thought God weighed the good things I did against the evil things. As long as the positive outweighed the negative, I would be acceptable to Him. I could not have been more wrong. The Word of God shows that His standard is perfection, and no matter how hard I tried, I could never achieve that goal.

1- Galatians 3:10–11: Establishes that anyone trying to keep the Law must keep all of the Law. Failure in any area means complete failure.

2- Romans 6:23: Records that the penalty for sin (any and all sin) is death. The old covenant reflects the same penalty for not living up to God's standard of perfection. "The soul that sinneth, it shall die" (Ezek. 18:4, 20).

3- Thinking ourselves to be "good enough" for God's presence is self-righteousness, which the Bible calls nothing but filthy rags (Isa. 64:6).

So much for trusting in that great balance scale in the sky!

We can never be good enough in our own strength to pass inspection in God's judgment.

In my not-always-humble opinion, the scariest Scripture in the Bible is found in Matthew 7:22–23. "Many will say to me in that day, Lord, Lord, have we not prophesied in thy name? and in thy name have cast out devils? and in thy name done many wonderful works? And then will I profess unto them, I never knew you: depart from me, ye that work iniquity."

Notice three important things in the above Scripture. The works that these people performed appear to be very spiritual activities, executed with apparent power, yet after spending their lives doing all kinds of good works, Jesus calls them evildoers and casts them out, stating He never knew them.

Objection #11—"Christianity is a crutch."

Pride is the apparent motivation behind this objection. The portrayal of Christianity has not reflected a glorious church without spot or wrinkle but rather a conglomerate of ignorant, uneducated, and weak-minded people. These follow a few flamboyant leaders who make money fleecing the flock. The concept of Christianity as a crutch originated with Karl Marx, a nineteenth-century socialist who coauthored *The Communist Manifesto*. His comment was about all religion, although Christianity appeared to be the main target. Marx said, "Religion is the opiate of the masses." He maintained that religion was an invention designed for people incapable of coping with the pressures of life. When this objection is raised, what is really being said is, "I am too strong to need Jesus." Simple observation of our society easily counters this argument. The fact is, these same prideful rejecters employ many crutches to sustain their emotions. Dependence on drugs, alcohol, tobacco, sex, money, power, material possessions, and codependence on others function as their crutches. Substitutions for a relationship with Jesus are pursued with the same fervor as the most devoted of worshippers.

Christians become strong by admitting their weakness and depending on God. Paul cites his own dependency in a letter to the Corinthian church. "But he said to me, 'My grace is sufficient for you, for my power is made perfect in weakness. Therefore I will boast all the more gladly about my weaknesses, so that Christ's power may rest on me. That is why, for Christ's sake, I delight in weaknesses, in insults, in hardships, in persecutions, in difficulties. For when I am weak, then I am strong'" (2 Cor. 12:9–10 NIV).

Objection #12—"I don't want to give up what I like doing."

There is no doubt that sin is pleasurable for a season or else why would we sin? The Bible reflects this in several Scriptures and also shows the progression of sin from temptation to death.

"But every man is tempted, when he is drawn away of his own lust, and enticed. Then when lust hath conceived, it bringeth forth sin: and sin, when it is finished, bringeth forth death" (James 1:14–15).

Sin is the separator responsible for the breach between God and man, requiring the extreme sacrifice of His only begotten Son to provide a way out. Those who say they do not want to give up what they are doing are making a dangerous choice. The objector knows that what he is doing is wrong, but he values it more than spending eternity with God. The best way to poke light into this dark world is to emphasize the gravity of his choice and the fact that God's love offers forgiveness. Be careful not to make light of the need for repentance. I have heard some propose that they would continue in their sin until they got old and then repent and become a Christian. When we consider that repentance is a gift of God, there is no guarantee that the objector will be able to repent when he is old. Death is not always for the elderly, nor does it always come with a warning.

"Do not be deceived, God is not mocked; for whatever a man sows, that he will also reap. For he who sows to his flesh will of the flesh reap corruption, but he who sows to the Spirit will of the Spirit reap everlasting life" (Gal. 6:7–8 NKJV).

"For what shall it profit a man, if he shall gain the whole world, and lose his own soul?" (Mark 8:36).

Someone once painted a word picture that illustrates how futile is the act of holding on to sin. The picture was of a stray dog intensely digging through a trash can and finding an old, rancid bone. He held the bone firmly in his mouth, refusing any attempt to remove it, even though it was not fit to eat. Someone offered the dog a sumptuous hunk of steak, hoping that such a tasty and nutritious meal would entice him to drop the old bone. The dog could not release what was harmful in order to receive what was good. The lesson of this word picture is that patience and prayer are essential in reaching those who cling to old bones.

Study/Teaching Outline—Your Honor, I Object!

Handling Common Objections
- The following questions are some of the most common objections people have to Christianity (suggested by a forum of pastors).
- The goal and benefit of studying these questions is to build your confidence by having a ready and short answer. These are not complete answers but only a direction-pointer to Jesus.
- Some practical hints: when answering a question, stick to the point! Jesus *is* the point, and so your purpose is always to point to Jesus.
- Don't be afraid to say you don't know the answer to a question.
- It is an opportunity to research and get back to the individual.

- Be attentive to the guidance off the Holy Spirit in giving your answer.
- Remember these short answers do not make you an expert but may allow you to redirect the conversation (point to Jesus).
- Any one of these questions, developed in depth, can fill up many hours.
- Your personal study on topics of interest is encouraged.
- Remember the real question is not always obvious.
- There are often questions behind the questions, reasons why people ask or respond the way they do in the first place. Be sensitive.
- If these are not casual contacts, try to find out what issues are stirring their souls and motivating them in the first place. This may open up a more effective witness opportunity.
- A biblical example is found in John 3. Nicodemus began his discussion with Jesus about miracles, but Jesus went right to the real need—becoming born again.

Class Discussion: For each of the following, discuss the answer given. Seek input from the students on variations of the question and variations on how it may be answered.

- Question 1. "I am an atheist. I don't believe in God" "I don't believe that God exists. How can anybody be sure?"
  - There are two kinds of skeptics: atheists and agnostics. Atheists say God doesn't exist, and agnostics say maybe God exists but we can't know anything about Him. Neither atheism nor agnosticism makes sense. (The Bible calls them fools in Psalm 14:1.)
  - Atheism requires complete knowledge of everything (which no human has). You have to know everything about everything to say there is no God.
  - Agnostics claim that they can't know anything for sure. (Note the contradiction: "One thing I know about God: you can't know anything about Him.")

- Possible motivation behind the question: if there is no God then there is no right and wrong, and I am not accountable for my sin. (Be aware of this possible motivation.)
  - Simple response: There is a "first, original, and primary cause."
- The evidence for God's existence.
- Every effect has a cause. Both science and the Bible acknowledge that the universe had a beginning and that it couldn't have arrived without a force behind it.
- Every creation has a creator. Nature itself points toward its Creator and reveals what He is like (Ps. 19:1).
- Every design has a designer. The intricate designs all around you, from the patterns of the universe to the uniqueness of a DNA strand, show that they must have resulted from an intelligent designer, rather than just random occurrence.
- Communication requires a communicator. The cells in people's bodies are filled with complex instructions that were programmed by someone intelligent to communicate that information to other cells (example: neurons, neurotransmitters).
- Every law has a lawgiver. The universal moral law of what's right and what's wrong crosses cultures, and must have come from an outside source. There is a "someone" who gave all humans a conscience (Rom. 2:14–15).
- Turning the conversation to Jesus. Nobody except Jesus has been able to keep the moral code perfectly. This shows that all humans need forgiveness and are in need of a Savior (2 Cor. 5:21).
  - God is knowable. God not only exists, but He created people in His image. He created us with wills, emotions, personalities, and ambitions. Since we are in His image, He must possess the same qualities as His creation.
  - God reveals Himself to the world so He can be sought. People are to seek Him and know Him. He promises that if they do, they'll find Him (Jer. 29:13).

Question #2. "What about evolution? Doesn't that contradict creation?"

- Background: Several generations have been taught that evolution was a fact, when it is (and has been) only an unproved theory. There are many good websites with detailed and useful information. Here are a few general points that will help you answer questions.
  - Why isn't creation taught in schools?
    - Because the rest of the world teaches evolution, scientists believe today's student will have large gaps of knowledge, and the US education system will fall behind the rest of the Western world if they are not taught that all species evolved. Therefore, they continue to propagate a dubious theory as fact.
  - Establishing a religion.
    - Some claim that teaching creation versus evolution would be establishing Judeo-Christian principles over other religions. If teachers taught a religious sampling of all different viewpoints of the creation story, they would have no time to teach anything else. (Truth is ignored simply because it is God's truth.)
- After two hundred years of Darwinism, the only thing that has evolved is the beliefs about evolution. As one false theory is proved impossible, another one is generated from the trash heap.
- Simple facts for a simple conclusion: evolution theory offers no proof or facts, just conjecture.
  - The fossil record shows no intermediate forms indicating a process of evolving into new species (no missing links).
  - The earth's surface is deposited in layers, and there are species found that span several geological layers (no evolving demonstrated here).
  - Animals appear suddenly at the start of the Cambrian Period. Only a few primitive multicellular fossils appear in earlier rock layers. The earth's fossil record reveals that every living form appeared suddenly and completely developed, not through gradual transition.
- God's special creation remains the only scientifically viable explanation for the origin of life and all biological designs.

Keep Your Answers Simple.

- Keep your response humble and simple. Acknowledge that species have physically adapted over time to survive but did not form entirely new species. Claims of the theory of evolution that those adaptations can actually result in the creation of new species are not supported by fact.
- Some other false theories you should know about:
  - Life itself randomly evolved from nonliving material. Given the complexity of life, the mathematical probability of life evolving at random is absurd.
  - Life came from chemical "ooze." Current research in molecular biology has revealed that proteins and nucleic acids are too structurally complex to have arisen spontaneously in the same place at the same time. The amino acids in DNA are also so complex, that they couldn't have begun by chance. So life could not have originated solely by chemical means.
- Accepting the theory of evolution requires faith, just as believing in creationism does. It's irrational to believe that something can randomly come from nothing, that order came out of chaos, and that lifeless matter produced conscious life.

Question #3. "How do I know the Bible is really true? What about errors and contradictions? The Bible is filled with errors."

- This is probably one of my favorite questions to answer using another question. "Have you ever read the Bible?"
  - Most will say they have not or have only read parts of it.
  - What most people claim as errors in the Bible aren't errors but translation or cultural difficulties.
  - People think they've stumbled upon apparent inconsistencies when they haven't taken the time to find out all the facts or made an in-depth study of the passage.
  - Many difficult questions in the Bible have been answered by new discoveries in fields such as language (word usage), history, archeology, and other sciences.

- The Bible is God's Word, and God cannot lie (Isa. 55:10–11; John 17:17; Titus 1:2; Heb. 4:12).
- Regardless of the kind of difficulty found, further study has always reconciled what appears to be error.
    - In the original language, the Bible is free from any error. This is called "inerrancy."
    - God's Word is described as "the word of truth" (2 Cor. 6:7; Col. 1:5; 2 Tim. 2:15; James 1:18).
    - "Inerrancy" (no errors in the Bible) isn't a theory about the Bible; it's the teaching of the Bible itself.
- A related logical question is "Why do we have so many different versions?"
    - Original languages are not used by most of the world's population (Hebrew, Aramaic, Greek); therefore, the originals have been translated into the common language of the nation.
    - Note: In a good translation, the validity of every word can be checked against the originals.
    - Nontranslations: Modern English-speaking countries have produced paraphrases to make the Bible more "user-friendly." These are not translations and have to be considered as *not* the inerrant Word of God. *Know what you are reading!*
    - To check your Bible, read the publisher's notes to see if it is a translation or a paraphrase or something else.
    - The further away from the original language, the less you can rely on the accuracy.
    - There are many good books that explore so-called "Bible difficulties." One is *Encyclopedia of Bible Difficulties* (G. Archer, 1982).

Question #4. "Why is there evil in the world? What about suffering? If God is so good, why is there evil?"

- The question behind this question may not be a question at all but deep-seated hurt.
  - ◦ Be sensitive to what the person is really saying, and look for areas to minister to the hurt after you have successfully answered the question.
- The base question is, how can the presence of evil be consistent with the God of the Bible?
  - ◦ God didn't create evil. God saw everything, and it was good (Gen 1:25, 31).
  - ◦ Evil is a result of sin, and sin entered the world through man's disobedience (Gen. 3).
  - ◦ The corruption brought about by sin is the reason for evil.
- Evil is necessary for free will. It gives humans the opportunity to make wrong choices.
- God has the solution for evil. He sent his Son, Jesus, to accomplish the ultimate defeat of evil on the cross.

Did God create evil as Isaiah 45:7 seems to indicate?

- Example of translation difficulty:
  - ◦ Isaiah 45:7 in the King James Version of the Bible seems to say that God created evil. However, the Hebrew word translated as "evil" has several other meanings that better fit the context of this chapter.
  - ◦ Possible translations of the Hebrew word used in other English translations are adversity, affliction, calamity, distress, disaster.
  - ◦ Translators of these later English Bibles chose to use the alternatives, since the idea that God created moral evil is contrary to the whole context of Scripture.

Why doesn't God just destroy all evil?

- God's timing. Just as we don't yet have eternal bodies, evil has yet to be removed from the world.

- Related question: "Why is there suffering?" Related answer: because of sin.
  - If Adam had not sinned, there would be no suffering and no death. "For as in Adam all die, In Christ shall all be made alive" (1 Cor. 15:22).
- The heart of this issue is the charge that God isn't fair. In our society, pleasure is a chief goal in life, closely followed by entertainment. This is called hedonism, and hedonists find any form of suffering offensive.
  - To say God isn't fair is an *extremely dangerous charge*.
  - If God gave us what we deserve, we'd be in deep trouble. We need to ask God for mercy and not justice.
  - God's mercy and grace are so taken for granted that suffering and pain shock us.
  - The epitome of suffering: consider the innocent sufferings of Jesus at Calvary. He took what we deserved.
    "He is despised and rejected of men; a man of sorrows, and acquainted with grief: and we hid as it were our faces from him; he was despised, and we esteemed him not. Surely he hath borne our griefs, and carried our sorrows: yet we did esteem him stricken, smitten of God, and afflicted. But he was wounded for our transgressions, he was bruised for our iniquities: the chastisement of our peace was upon him; and with his stripes we are healed" (Isa. 53:3–5).

Question #5. "Is hell for real? Why would a loving God send people there?"
(Closely related to the suffering question.)
- While evil and suffering and pain are very real, they are also very temporary.
  - When God deals with evil, He will deal with *all evil*. In the meantime, God desires as many people as possible to accept Jesus's death and resurrection as payment for their sins, so they can live eternally with him.

- Hell is a choice. The sad fact is, many make the decision not to accept God's way and be a part of God's heaven. God doesn't send them to hell; they send themselves.
- Hell was created for the Devil and his angels. Those refusing to accept God's solution to sin will join them there by their own choice.
- Some do not fear hell because they think it is just a big immoral party to be shared with their friends. Nothing could be further from truth.
- Quote for discussion: "For God to force people to go to heaven against their wishes wouldn't be heaven—it would be hell. The gates of hell are locked from the inside by the free choice of men and women."—atheist author Jean-Paul Sartre

Question #6. "What about the people who never heard the gospel? Do they go to hell?"
- Most of the time, the real motivation behind this question is to prove that God is unjust and to get the heat off themselves.
  ○ Let's shift the conversation and talk about how God deals with other people and not me.
- Remember that the Holy Spirit convicts of sin and righteousness, and that can be uncomfortable.
  ○ Don't let the person off the hook unless led by the Holy Spirit. Answer the question; then come back to them with a "What about you?" question.
- What does the Bible say about those who've never had the opportunity to hear about Jesus?
  ○ They are judged according to the light they have. Romans 2:11–16 speaks about how they will be judged according to the law that is written in their hearts. The law written in their hearts is the knowledge of right and wrong and the testimony of nature.
  ○ God will do what is right, and the only way to have your sins forgiven is through Jesus.
  ○ An important biblical principle to understand is that no one has ever remained lost who wanted to be found. Wanting to

be found is being drawn by God Himself. Just as God sent the apostle Philip to the seeking Ethiopian, Jesus promises all who seek will find (Acts 8:26–39; Matt. 7:7–8).

- ◦ Current example: Many living in Islamic countries who never heard the gospel report having dreams and visions of Jesus that led them to salvation.

- Important turn-around to point to Jesus: Like Abraham said, "Shall not the judge of all the earth do right?" (Gen 18:25). Remind the questioner that he has no excuse. He has had the opportunity to hear the gospel, and so will be held accountable by God for the light he has been given. Keep the heat on! Your job is to point to Jesus, not to make him comfortable in his sin.

Question #5. All religions are the same. "Aren't there many roads to heaven? Don't all paths ultimately lead to the same place?" We all worship the same God, as long as you are sincere!

- All religions are not the same, but many share similar ethics (standards of right and wrong).
  - ◦ We call these Judeo-Christian principles. Ethics are not the same as faith.
- Unlike all other religions, Christianity alone has a founder who overcame death and who promises that His followers will do the same.
  - ◦ Jesus is alive. All other religions were founded by men and prophets whose end was the grave. Over five hundred eyewitnesses testified to the risen Jesus (1 Cor. 15:6). This evidence would be admissible in any court.
  - ◦ As Christians, we take comfort in the fact that our God became a man, died for our sins, was crucified, and was resurrected the third day. The grave could not hold Him. He lives, and He sits today at the right hand of God the Father in heaven.
  - ◦ The living church has a living head. This is unique to Christianity.
- Jesus said He was the only way to come to the Father (John 14:6).

- Peter affirmed this teaching when he made reference to fact that Jesus was the one the prophets foretold and that there is no other name by which we can be saved (Acts 4:12).
- Paul echoed the same doctrine, writing to Timothy that Jesus is the only mediator between God and mankind (1 Tim. 2:5).

"But all God expects of us is sincerity. I am doing the best I can, and I'm sincere."

- Even if you do your very best it is not good enough to please God. His standard is perfection.
  ◦ If doing your sincere best were good enough, then Jesus would not have had to die on the cross (Gal. 2:21).
- Sincerity is not the way to heaven. What if you are sincerely wrong?
- If you are relying on your sincerity, then you are saying you are good enough, on your own, to be with God. This is called self-righteousness.
- Sincerity is not enough. You must have faith in the salvation provided through Jesus.

Related question: Isn't it enough just to do whatever I feel is right?

- Have your feelings ever turned out to be wrong?
- Your feelings do not determine truth. The Bible tells us our hearts (feelings) are deceitful (Jer. 17:9). We are not to lean to our own understanding (Prov. 3:5–6).
- If faith is based on what you feel is right, then what if some people felt stealing was acceptable?
  ◦ Could you trust someone who believed in a religion that felt it was all right to steal, lie, kill, and cheat?
- Hitler felt killing Jews was right. He was wrong. Radical Islamists believe it is right to kill innocents if it causes terror for their cause. They are wrong.
- The Bible has revealed that only God is the source of truth and not your feelings.
  ◦ A carpenter will use a measure to determine the true length of the board he will cut. If he is smart, he will measure

twice and cut once. In the same manner, the Bible is our measure, our standard of right and wrong. Double check your thoughts and plans against the truth of God's Word.

- ○ Circumstances do not affect absolute truth.
- ○ Real truth will not contradict itself. If someone felt that something was right and another person felt it was wrong, they cannot both be right.

Question #6. "Christians are all hypocrites. Why would I want to be one? The Christians I know aren't much different from anyone else."

- Be aware that this question may mask deep hurts suffered at the hands of the church or at the hands of supposed Christians. *Handle with gentleness.*
- What is a hypocrite? A hypocrite is an actor, a person who pretends to be something he isn't. Jesus had hard words for hypocrites (Matt. 23:27).
  - ○ In reality, there always has been and always will be some hypocrites in the church. But Jesus doesn't ask us to follow others; he asks us to follow Him.
  - ○ The real question isn't whether there are hypocrites in the church but whether Jesus is a hypocrite.
- The Bible presents Jesus as perfect and without sin of any kind (2 Cor. 5:21).
  - ○ Jesus's disciples testified that Jesus was without sin (1 Peter 2:22; 1 John 3:5).
  - ○ Even Jesus Himself challenged others to prove that He'd ever sinned (John 8:46).
- What about the atrocities supposedly committed by Christians?
  - ○ Some blame Christianity for religious wars like the Crusades, burning witches, the Inquisition, slavery, even the Holocaust.
  - ○ The responsibility for atrocities is an extension of the question of hypocrites. So-called "believers" (who didn't practice true Christianity) did practice evil.
  - ○ In reality, many of these people were Christian in name only. (Hitler may have been a Catholic, but he certainly

was not a Christian. This does not mean that all Catholics are not Christian.)

  ○ Focusing on atrocities committed by false Christians is a smokescreen to avoid the real issue of personal sin.

- Many more positive achievements than negative actions are the result of Christianity. Christians established numerous hospitals, schools, colleges, orphanages, relief agencies, and charities. No other religion in history can compare (James 1:26–27).

Question #7. "I don't think I'm a sinner. I'm not so bad." (The love of sinning)

- The question of personal sin goes to the heart of why we need a Savior. Recognizing that we are sinners is the gateway to salvation.

  ○ If sin is not recognized and acknowledged, there is no repentance and no salvation.

- How we recognize sin.

  ○ Ask if the person knows what sin is. (The answer is, falling short of God's standard as expressed in His Law.)

  ○ God's standards are not only for Jews but for the whole world.

  ○ Here are some Scriptures that support this definition. "Now we know that whatever the law says, it says to those who are under the law, so that every mouth may be silenced and the whole world held accountable to God. Therefore no one will be declared righteous in God's sight by the works of the law; rather, through the law we become conscious of our sin" (Rom. 3:19–20 NIV).

- Everyone who breaks God's law is a sinner by definition. "Everyone who sins breaks the law; in fact, sin is lawlessness" (1 John 3:4 NIV).

- God gave us the Law to show us that we are sinners in need of a savior. Paul calls the Law a "tutor." "Therefore the law was our tutor to bring us to Christ, that we might be justified by faith" (Gal. 3:24 NKJV).

- ○ Paul affirms that without the Law, even he would not have known what sin was. "What shall we say then? Is the law sin? God forbid. Nay, I had not known sin, but by the law: for I had not known lust, except the law had said, Thou shalt not covet" (Rom. 7:7).
- Conclusion: The Law leaves us guilty before the Lord, who judges righteously.
- To demonstrate that the person claiming he is not a sinner really doesn't know what sin is:
  You might ask if he can name the Ten Commandments. (If he does not know God's Law, he will not see sin as sinful.)
  - ○ When the Law is not known, he is not in a position to say he is not a sinner.
  - ○ FYI: There are excellent videos available on the Internet addressing sin. A good one is *Hell's Best Kept Secret* from Ray Comfort and Kirk Cameron.

Related question: "I am not as bad as others. I do plenty of good works. Doesn't that outweigh the bad I have done?"

- Many have the mistaken view that God's judgment takes the form of a giant balance scale in the sky, in which good works will be balanced against bad deeds. This is false. The Bible says:
  - ○ the wages of sin [any and all sin] is death (Rom. 6:23).
  - ○ The soul that sins shall die (Ezek. 18:4, 20).
- No one can keep the Law and no one has ever kept the Law except Jesus (Gal. 3:11).
  - ○ Jesus's perfection under the Law: "For He made Him who knew no sin to be sin for us, that we might become the righteousness of God in Him" (2 Cor. 5:21).
- The Bible calls our so-called good works "filthy rags" (Isa. 64:6).
- Something scary will happen to those who trust in their good works instead of a covenant relationship with Jesus Christ. "Many will say to me on that day, 'Lord, Lord, did we not prophesy in your name and in your name drive out demons and in your name perform many miracles?' Then I will tell them

plainly, 'I never knew you. Away from me, you evildoers!'"
(Matt. 7:22–23 NIV).

- ◦ Notice all the spiritual-sounding good works done by these people.
- ◦ Notice Jesus says He never knew them!
- ◦ Notice Jesus calls them "evildoers."
- ◦ So much for thinking good works make a difference in salvation.

Related topic: Christianity is a crutch.

- • Karl Marx, author of *The Communist Manifesto*, said, "Religion is the opiate of the masses."[4]
- • Marx charged that religion is an invention designed for people incapable of coping with life's pressures, therefore Christianity is just "a crutch.
  - ◦ Prideful people maintain they don't need this type of emotional crutch.
  - ◦ However, other emotional crutches are very apparent among those rejecting Christianity because it is a crutch.
  - ◦ Dependence on drugs, alcohol, tobacco, sex, money, power, other people, and material possessions are used to cope with life's pressures.
- • On the contrary, Christians become strong in their weakness because they depend on God. "That is why, for Christ's sake, I delight in weaknesses, in insults, in hardships, in persecutions, in difficulties. For when I am weak, then I am strong" (2 Cor. 12:10 NIV).

---

[4] Marx, Karl. 1844 *A Contribution to the Critique of Hegel's* Philosophy of Right, *Deutsch-Französische Jahrbücher,* February.

CHAPTER NINE

Another Jesus; Another Gospel

W hen I consider the technologically advanced world in which we live, the marvelous developments in communication, and the almost instant access to libraries of information, I cannot help but marvel. I was a young adult, sitting next to my elderly grandmother, watching the TV coverage of Neil Armstrong's walk on the moon. I was fascinated to see travel to the moon, but it had an even greater impact on my grandmother. Something she said has stayed in my mind all these years. "When I was a girl, the only way to travel was to walk or by horse-drawn cart. Now I have seen men travel to the moon." She then expressed that she no longer felt part of this world. Other than her disengagement with modernity, what registered with me about her comment was the degree of progress that had happened in just one lifetime.

I too have seen tremendous technological developments in my lifetime. While daily living got easier, the spiritual climate seems to have become darker and colder, almost in negative correlation to scientific advances. When I consider the failure to recognize basic biblical right and wrong, that we murder our unborn children in the womb and sanction sodomy and sexual promiscuity of all descriptions, I understand how Granny felt. My question is, "Where are the children of God? Why isn't the church of Jesus Christ making a stand?" It is no wonder that the Enemy is at our gate, making inroads with terrorist attacks. We are just like Israel prior to being given over to her enemies because we have wandered so far from the Lord.

When there are acts of violence in the nation, or the media reports a scandal, the common remedy proposed is the removal of Constitutional rights and more education. "Restrict and educate, and we will eradicate the evil" is the politically acceptable outcry. Did you ever wonder why the high level of education readily available to our generation hasn't improved us spiritually? If education was the answer, why hasn't cultural morality progressed beyond less-literate centuries? But it is obvious that the spiritual condition of mankind has not progressed and in fact is growing worse. Paul identified our society more than two thousand years ago. His prophecy concerning end times seems to be coming true every day.

"But know this, that in the last days perilous times will come: For men will be lovers of themselves, lovers of money, boasters, proud, blasphemers, disobedient to parents, unthankful, unholy, unloving, unforgiving, slanderers, without self-control, brutal, despisers of good, traitors, headstrong, haughty, lovers of pleasure rather than lovers of God, having a form of godliness but denying its power" (2 Tim. 3:1–5 NKJV).

"But evil men and impostors will grow worse and worse, deceiving and being deceived." (2 Tim.3:13 NKJV).

For most of us, we can only serve the Lord in our own generation, and this is the nature of the generation to which you and I have been called. You are chosen to serve now! Be alert, and be aware of opportunities to make a difference.

How to Reach Those in Other Religions

Now that you have been "activated" and are aware of the potential harvest right outside your door, don't be surprised when the Lord answers your prayer and put all kinds of people in your path. Sometimes those people will be from a background very different from your own. When Paul and Barnabas set out on their missionary journeys to unreached areas, they came into contact with people who worshipped a variety of false gods and even some who openly practiced witchcraft. Occasionally, they revisited areas where they had established a church to see how the work was progressing. They found some churches had been deceived, drifting into false doctrines that threatened the truth of the gospel that they had preached to them.

Your missionary activities will bring you into contact with similar challenges. You will encounter people enslaved to false gods, some practicing New Age techniques that are really a form of witchcraft and some who are devotees of Christian-sounding cults that have invented another Jesus and another gospel. The names and faces of the false gods Paul faced may have changed, but the same spiritual entity is operating behind the scenes. Truly, we are not wrestling against flesh and blood but principalities and powers whose objective is to cloud the truth of the gospel of Jesus Christ with all sorts of falsehood.

Broad Strokes and Red Flags

Since the variety of the false is so vast, I think the most productive approach is to identify and study the common areas the Enemy attacks, rather than the numerous organizations that are perpetrating the counterfeit teachings. When you have a firm grip on what the Bible says, the spotlight of the Holy Spirit will reveal the handiwork of the adversary who is working to steal, kill, and destroy. Counterfeits are best spotted by intimately knowing the real thing.

Counterfeits come in various "flavors." They can appear as an entirely different religion such as Buddhism, Hinduism, or Islam. They can also appear as Christian-sounding cults that pervert the cardinal doctrines of the Bible. Do not confuse these cults with Christian denominations that maintain the essentials of biblical teaching but vary in tradition and practice. When talking with a person of another faith, it is okay to ask him about what he believes and what he believes about Jesus. Here are some areas to help you spot the essentials. Use it as an outline for your conversation. It may help you to build a bond with a true brother of another denomination, or it may show you where you must direct a pinpoint of light into darkness. These are the areas that Satan, the author of lies, loves to use to confuse.

1- The deity of Jesus.
2- Jesus's relationship to the Father. (Is He the only begotten Son?)

3- How to get saved. (Adding to God's grace. What other things are needed?)

4- Is there another mediator besides Jesus?

5- Other sources of authority besides the Word of God.

6- There is no sin. There is no hell.

7- Allegiance to a charismatic personality instead of Jesus.

Who Is Jesus?

The answer to this question will reveal the center of a person's belief system. Jesus is given honorable mention in several major religions, but the answer to the question, "Who is He?" reveals how great the deception can be, while still sounding "religious." For example, Buddhism and its derivatives define Jesus as a man who achieved an enlightened state, an ascended master. Islam acknowledges Jesus as a prophet but not the Son of God. Inside that expensive gold-domed building situated on the Temple Mount in Jerusalem is an inscription that quotes the Quran, stating that Allah has not begotten and that he has no partner. Other inscriptions mention Jesus as a prophet, a messenger of Allah. Their answer is plain. Their Jesus is not the Jesus of the Bible. Never let anyone tell you that we worship the same god as the Muslims.

"Who is a liar but he who denieth that Jesus is the Christ? He is antichrist who denieth the Father and the Son. Whosoever denieth the Son, the same hath not the Father: [but] he that acknowledgeth the Son hath the Father also" (1 John 2:22–23).

"He that believeth on the Son of God hath the witness in himself: he that believeth not God hath made him a liar; because he believeth not the record that God gave of his Son" (1 John 5:10).

"For God so loved the world that he gave his only begotten Son, that whosoever believeth in him should not perish, but have everlasting life … He who believes in Him is not condemned; but he who does not believe is condemned already, because he has not believed in the name of the only begotten Son of God" (John 3:16, 18).

Simply put, whatever label is worn by the proponent of the belief system, if there is no acknowledgement, such as made by Peter, you are dealing with a counterfeit religion.

"And Simon Peter answered and said, Thou art the Christ, the Son of the living God" (Matt. 16:16).

Speak the Truth in Love

Our politically correct culture pressures us to accept all religions as equal. While we want to be gracious to other religions, we cannot accept them as valid. If we do this, we mask the Enemy's lies that hold millions of souls in bondage. While we strive to enhance our image and say nice things about them, their adherents continue to race toward an eternity separated from Christ. Of course, we need to be loving in spirit, but we also need to expose the lie and speak the truth. Remember the job of Satan is to steal, to kill, and to destroy (John 10:10). You must speak the truth!

Judaism

Judaism must be addressed. Right now, religious Jews are still looking for the promised Messiah but discount Jesus of Nazareth as fulfilling that promise. Few Jews are well acquainted with their own scriptures but maintain cultural identity through tradition. It is possible to reach Jews through several of those traditions, especially Passover, which actually speaks of Jesus. If your Jewish friend is acquainted with the Tanakh (the Hebrew bible), there are many avenues of approach. One of my favorites is Daniel's seventieth week, which historically dates the Messiah's entry into Jerusalem on the very day we call Palm Sunday (Dan. 9:24–26). Judaism is the root of Christianity, and we have been grafted into the root of that tree. Paul tells us that a temporary blindness has come over the natural descendants of Abraham. Romans 11:25 maintains that there will come a time when that blindness will be removed, and the Jews will once again be grafted back into the tree of belief. If the Lord frequently puts Jewish people into your path, remember they have historically not been treated with love by Christian cultures. Defense walls may be in place to an even greater degree than others you encounter. Change that perspective with your love. Poking a little light into the darkness, coupled with your prayer, is always the answer. There are many wonderful ministries that can provide you with materials on how the spiritual children of Abraham (the church) can reach out to his natural seed. One of these ministries was very instrumental in my own salvation experience.

In ministering to those who identify themselves as believers in any other faith, offer the hope we have in Jesus Christ to spend eternity in His loving presence and in the presence of the Father as His beloved children. Try to remember that no matter how passionately they hold to their beliefs, they are victims of deception of the Evil One. You have the truth, the only truth (John 14:6). Never argue! Share Jesus with love and humility. Don't be discouraged if you are not the one to harvest; just continue planting and watering.

Islam—A New Frontier

A new challenge for Christians in Western cultures is the religion of Islam. Most of us have not interacted with Muslims to any extent, and so outreach to people of that culture has only recently become an issue. Islam is a constantly growing force in the world, if only for the reason that Muslims tend to have very many children. As of 2001, followers of Islam accounted for 22 percent of the world's population, so the harvest field is vast. Few of us know anything at all about these folks, except that some of their women dress differently and, for the most part, they do not mix socially with non-Muslims. How do we reach these precious souls for the Lord Jesus Christ when there are obvious walls up on both sides of the faith issue? Let's try to cut through those walls by learning a little about Islam and the areas where the light of Jesus Christ will be most effective in penetrating the darkness.

Some Basics

At first glance, there seem to be many similarities between Christianity and Islam. Familiar stories, with a few slight twists, and familiar names from the Bible reinforce the assertion of similarity. However, upon closer examination, the vast spiritual difference between the two faiths becomes obvious.

You may have heard that Muslims worship the same God as Christians and Jews, but that is not the case. While it is true that all three faiths believe there is only one God (monotheism), the nature of the Christian God is very different from that of the Allah of Islam. Islam recognizes many of the prophets, such as Adam, Moses, and Abraham, and even reverences a person called Jesus, the son of Mary. In Muslim literature, Jesus is called "Isa."

There are two main source books treasured by Muslims that speak of Isa. The first is the Quran, which provides a history of his life, and the second, called the Hadith, is a collection of Muhammad's words and deeds as remembered by his followers, a century or two after his death. The Hadith discusses Isa's place in what Muslims believe will be the future. One thing is clear: the Isa of Islam is not the Jesus of the gospels. Muslims believe Jesus was a created being, sent as a messenger of Allah to teach obedience. They believe he was born of a virgin and performed great miracles, even raising the dead, yet like Adam, he was only a man. The Islamic holy book, the Quran, states the following, concerning the claims that Jesus is the Son of God.

"It is not befitting to [the majesty of] Allah that He should beget a son. Glory be to Him! When He determines a matter, He only says to it, 'Be,' and it is" (Quran 19:35, Yusif Ali Version).

Note: The Quran pronounces the curse of Allah on anyone who says that Jesus is the Son of God.

Partial Crucifixion but No Resurrection

Muslims do not believe that Jesus died on the cross. They acknowledge that He was crucified, but believe He was whisked off the cross before death and taken to heaven. The body hanging on the cross thought to be Jesus was replaced, probably by Judas Iscariot (Quran 4:157–8). Because He did not really die on the cross, there was no need for a resurrection. Muslims believe that Jesus will return to the earth prior to the final judgment and affirm Islam as the true religion. At the final judgment, Jesus will be a witness against Christians and Jews who believed in His death and resurrection. In fact, according to the Hadith, Isa will have a very important role in end-time events. He will not only establish Islam as the one true faith but also make war until He destroys all other religions except Islam (Quran 4:159).

No Atonement Needed

The removal of Jesus from the cross in Muslim teaching is not a surprise when the nature of Islam is explained. Islam does not require an atoning sacrifice for sin. Islam is a works-centered religion, and salvation is earned by doing good works. They believe that on judgment day, all works will be accounted for, and if the individual's good deeds outnumber his or her evil ones, the individual may have a chance to enter heaven. Muslims believe that Allah is sovereign but not immutable. He can and does change his mind. It is possible to be considered righteous according to your works and still end up in hell, if Allah wills it. It seems that Allah can be capricious. There is also a kind of temporary hell in Muslim teaching, where sins can be burned off. After spending time burning in Islamic purgatory, entrance into heaven may be gained, when and if Allah wills it.

The only people guaranteed heaven in Islamic teaching are those engaged in jihad. Jihad literally means "exerting force for Allah." Westerners interpret jihad to be the root cause of terrorist acts perpetrated against our civilization, but it can simply mean evangelizing for Islam or even writing a book for Allah. Unfortunately, some radicals see a violent death as a quicker path to heaven. Our generation has seen a proliferation of young men and women willing to die for Islam, taking as many other innocent and unsuspecting people with them as they possibly can.

I once attended a lecture about the teachings of Islam conducted by a Lebanese Christian who grew up in a predominantly Muslim community. A common teaching in some Muslim circles is that those who enter paradise will be given seventy virgins for eternal company. A problem that is never discussed with potential jihadists is the ambiguity of the Arabic characters expressing this promise. Scholars are not sure what is meant by the character following the one meaning "seventy." According to the instructor, the Arabic characters translated as seventy "virgins" is quite unclear and can also be correctly translated as seventy "grapes." Though this may bring a smile to your face, it is truly sad. It also highlights a fertile area for witnessing. Christians have a sure promise of salvation through the atoning sacrifice of Jesus Christ, and our promised reward is also sure. Where He is, we shall be also (John 14:3).

How Muslims View Christians

The negative view of Western culture held by Muslims is not entirely unjustified. Unfortunately, Muslim opinion paints Christians with the same brush as those who produce pornography, X-rated movies, and rude and uncouth TV shows. America is known as a Christian nation; therefore, everything produced in America is Christian, according to Muslim opinion. Frankly, the foul language and overt sexual nature of many shows in America make me cringe and turn off the TV, and I have had many years of viewing to become desensitized. To the Muslim world, there is no difference between a Christian in Duluth and a pornographer in Hollywood. "Christian" America is believed to be the source of free sex, rape, alcohol, and divorce. Is it any wonder we are called the "great Satan"? Becoming a friend to your Islamic neighbor, inviting him into your home and into your life, is a good way to demonstrate that what they have been taught about Christians is just not true.

What Muslims Believe about the Bible

Muslims think that Christians worship three gods: God the Father, God the Son, and Mary, the mother of God. They do not believe the Holy Bible is trustworthy because it has been changed by Jews and Christians. An example of something they believe the Jews have changed is the promise given to Abraham. Muslims believe the heir of all the promises of the book of Genesis was not Isaac but Ishmael, Abraham's son through Hagar, the Egyptian concubine. This is the crux of the whole controversy. They do believe in the prophets and the psalms of David, but again, they do not trust the Christian Scriptures. Muslims believe the Quran has superseded the Christian Scriptures. Witnessing to a Muslim through what the Bible teaches may be difficult, until the Holy Spirit reveals truth to his heart.

Reaching Your Muslim Neighbor

The starting point in your witness to a Muslim is not very different from any other unbeliever. Pray for the wisdom and guidance of the Holy Spirit, and pray specifically for the one God has put on your heart. Remember, it is the Father that draws a man or woman to Christ, so pray that God will use you to plant that seed, water that seed, or harvest. .

Be willing to become a friend. An important dynamic for a Muslim is a sense of belonging to a community. If a Muslim becomes a believer in Jesus Christ, it is a certainty that he will, at the very least, be ostracized from his family and friends. That is a very lonely and frightening place to be. Some Christian converts report that they stayed within the Muslim community for quite a while, even though they knew the truth, just to avoid the loss of society. A loving Christian social alternative makes the transition to truth a bit easier. Include your Muslim friend in as many social events as you can.

Be willing to listen to Muslim beliefs with courtesy and interest. When you speak of your own faith, stick to the cardinal doctrines of the faith, and respond to sincere questions. Remember to treat your Bible with respect. Don't toss it around or put it on the floor. Muslims are taught to physically revere the Quran, so mishandling the Holy Bible will reflect how you feel about God's Word in their eyes.

Above all, keep your focus on Jesus. Stressing the assurance of salvation we have because of His work and His resurrection will show your Muslim friend the hope you have for now and for eternity. Do not say anything negative about Allah or Mohammed, as this will likely cause a knee-jerk negative reaction, shutting down the door of communication. Share the plan of salvation, stressing that it is a gift from God and not something earned by good works. "For by grace are ye saved through faith; and that not of yourselves: it is the gift of God" (Eph. 2:8).

What Is a Christian Cult?

Remember the old expression, "If you can't beat them, join them"? That is an introduction to a Christian cult. A Christian cult is a group that claims to be Christian but deviates from the essential doctrines of faith, salvation, God, and Jesus Christ. There is often a strong charismatic leader of the cult who exercises control over followers. Examples of famous cult leaders are David Koresh of the Branch Davidians, Jim Jones of the People's Temple, Joseph Smith Jr. of the Mormons, Charles Taze Russell of Jehovah's Witnesses, and L. Ron Hubbard of Scientology.

I think those who are entrapped by a cult are among the saddest of people you will meet. Many are diligent and hardworking, trying to earn what is the free gift of God. It is easy for someone to get caught up in their zeal if that person does not know the truth of the Word. For a sample of what I am talking about, consider the Mormon's, formally known as the Church of Jesus Christ of Latter-day Saints (LDS). This is an aggressively evangelistic group, contending that it is the only true church, and that all Christians outside Mormonism are following a deficient gospel and a false Christ.

According to Mormon theology:

• Jesus is a created being, the literal offspring of God the Father and one of His heavenly wives.

- God the Father (Elohim) dwells on a planet with His many spirit wives, producing numerous spirit children, who wait to inhabit physical bodies so that they too may one day ascend to God status, as their parents did.
- Jesus is believed to be the firstborn spirit child of Elohim.
- One of Jesus's spiritual brothers was Lucifer.

Mormons are usually very moral and nice people who are deceived by false teaching. Without knowing the Word of God, it is possible that you too could be influenced by other sources and be deceived. Several other cults are discussed in the teaching outline following this chapter. Many are hungering after truth. Help them find it.

What Is the Occult?

The word occult comes from a Latin word meaning "hidden." Practicing the occult involves any attempt to gain supernatural powers or knowledge apart from the God of the Bible; for example, witchcraft, Satanism, psychic activities, astrology, séances, tarot cards, Ouija boards. Some groups blend Christian-sounding names and terms into their practices to disguise the true source of manifestations; for example, the Caribbean practices of Santeria. Santeria uses saints' names along with animal sacrifices, chants, and rituals in an attempt to contact God. The source of all these activities is Satan. These are not harmless games played by the curious. Any degree of success in occult practice brings greater and greater darkness and can lead to demonic possession.

Some occult practices avoid the flamboyance of overt satanic rituals. Practices like Wicca masquerade as nature-loving, mild forces for achieving harmony with nature. Their followers often call themselves "white witches" but in fact, Wicca comes in contact with the same old spirit of darkness behind other more gruesome kinds of occult practices.

In recent years, some Christian counselors have been using a practice known as theophostic prayer. When a person recalls a particularly painful life experience, he is encouraged to visualize Jesus in the situation with him. While this may sound okay initially, the problem is we cannot conjure up Jesus on demand. This too is a form of witchcraft. The apparitions of Jesus many report seeing are clever counterfeits, contrived by the Enemy. Beware of anyone who encourages you to engage in extra-biblical practices.

The Study/Teaching Outline for this chapter will expand exploration of the occult and hopefully prepare you for some of the challenges you may face. If you have studied the Word of God and if you have prayed for insight and guidance, you are ready to go and make disciples in your sphere of influence. Have you ever noticed the book of Acts of the Apostles doesn't really end? The followers of Jesus Christ in every generation are reaching out to make disciples of all nations. Every generation writes another chapter in the book of Acts. Begin writing your chapter today.

Study/Teaching Outline for Another Jesus, Another Gospel

How to Interact with "Christian" Cults, Other Religions, Other Christian Denominations

Counterfeits of Truth
- Other religions (other than Judaism) are products of distortion and lies of the Enemy.
- There is only one way, one truth, and one life, and Jesus is it (John 14:6).
- Remember, the job of Satan is to steal, to kill, and to destroy (John 10:10).
- We want to be nice and gracious to people who belong to other religions and cults, but we must not mask the lies of the enemy.
  - While we say "nice things" about them, the theologies, philosophies, and teachers of other religions and cults are leading countless numbers into an eternity without Jesus.
  - We need to lovingly expose the lie and speak the truth, no matter the cost. Paul said, "Am I therefore become your enemy, because I tell you the truth?" (Gal. 4:16).

Why is Judaism in a different category?

- Judaism is the root of Christianity. We (the church) are branches grafted on to the tree of Judaism. (Israel is often represented as an olive tree in Scripture.)

  If the part of the dough offered as firstfruits is holy, then the whole batch is holy; if the root is holy, so are the branches If some of the branches have been broken off, and you, though a wild olive shoot, have been grafted in among the others and now share in the nourishing sap from the olive root, do not consider yourself to be superior to those other branches. If you do, consider this: You do not support the root, but the root supports you. You will say then, "Branches were broken off so that I could be grafted in." Granted. But they were broken off because of unbelief, and you stand by faith. Do not be arrogant, but tremble. For if God did not spare the natural branches, he will not spare you either. (Rom. 11:16–21 NIV)

  ✓ Note: We are "grafted in" to the olive tree. We (the church) do not replace it.

- A temporary blindness has come over the Jewish people so that the gospel can be preached to the Gentile nations (Rom. 11:25).

- Some Jews become believers now; they become part of the church.

  ◦ Prophecy tells us the Jews will accept the Lord when He is revealed to them at the end of the age.

    "And so all Israel will be saved; just as it is written, 'the deliverer will come from Zion, he will remove ungodliness from Jacob.' This is my covenant with them, when I take away their sins" (Rom. 11:26–27).

- Note: Only Jesus can save; therefore, Jewish people are not saved by being Jewish, only by coming to know Jesus as Messiah. *But* God has not forgotten his promise to Abraham, Isaac, and Jacob. He has not forsaken the Jews.

- There is a great deal of abuse to overcome in evangelizing Jewish people because many have attributed anti-Jewish atrocities to the Christians. (Some even think Hitler was a Christian.)

  ◦ Treat them with love and understanding and show them Jesus through your love and their own scriptures. (That's how Paul approached the Jews.)

Common Areas of Attack; The Enemy Counterfeits the Truth

- Other religions as well as Christian cults have a common source—Satan, who comes to steal to kill and to destroy (John 10:10).
- These groups differ from one another in how they attack, but the goal and target is the same.
- Typical areas of truth attacked by the Enemy in order to deceive
  - The deity of Jesus
  - Jesus's relationship to God the Father
  - How to get saved (adding to God's grace; other things you must do)
  - Another mediator besides Jesus
  - Other sources of authority besides the Word of God
  - There is no sin; there is no hell.
  - Allegiance to a charismatic personality other than Jesus
- Paul exposed the source of those who were changing the truth of his message.

"The god of this age has blinded the minds of unbelievers, so that they cannot see the light of the gospel that displays the glory of Christ, who is the image of God. For what we preach is not ourselves, but Jesus Christ as Lord, and ourselves as your servants for Jesus' sake" (2 Cor. 4:4–5 NIV).

"For if someone comes to you and preaches a Jesus other than the Jesus we preached, or if you receive a different spirit from the Spirit you received, or a different gospel from the one you accepted, you put up with it easily enough" (2 Cor. 11:4 NIV).

"I marvel that ye are so soon removed from him that called you into the grace of Christ unto another gospel: Which is not another; but there be some that trouble you, and would pervert the gospel of Christ. But though we, or an angel from heaven, preach any other gospel unto you than that which we have preached unto you, let him be accursed. As we said before, so say I now again, if any man preach any other gospel unto you than that ye have received, let him be accursed" (Gal. 1:6–9).

✓   Note: It is vital that we know the Word of God so that we will not be deceived.

What Is a "Christian" Cult?
- Definition: "cult" refers to a group that claims to be Christian but deviates from the essential doctrines of faith, salvation, God, and Jesus Christ.
- Cult leaders often exercise strong and destructive authority over their followers (examples: Branch Davidians; Jim Jones and the People's Temple).
  ◦ For our purposes, a cult is defined as a counterfeit form of Christianity, deviating from biblical doctrine and exercising destructive authority over followers.
- Scripture warns us about Satan's counterfeiting what God has said and done. "Be sober, be vigilant; because your adversary the devil, as a roaring lion, walketh about seeking whom he may devour" (1 Peter 5:8).
- There are numerous cults in the United States, and more form each year. Some that you may be familiar with are Mormonism, Scientology, Jehovah's Witnesses, the Aryan Brotherhood, and the Black Muslims.
  ◦ The following is only a sample of deceptive and destructive beliefs incorporated in the teachings of the cults.
  ◦ The examples show how the enemy attacks and perverts the gospel, keeping millions from the truth.
- The Church of Jesus Christ of Latter-day Saints (Mormonism). Started in 1830 by Joseph Smith, this aggressively evangelistic group contends that it is the only true church and that all Christians outside Mormonism are following a false Christ and a false gospel.
  ◦ What Mormon doctrine says about Jesus: Jesus is a created being, the literal offspring of God the Father and one of His heavenly wives.

- ° According to Mormon theology, God the Father (Elohim) dwells on a planet with his many spirit wives, producing numerous spirit children who await to inhabit physical bodies so that they too may one day ascend to "God" status, as their parents did. Jesus is believed to be the firstborn spirit child of Elohim.
  - ° According to Mormon theology, one of Jesus's spiritual brothers was Lucifer.
- Contrast false Mormon belief with the truth of Scripture: John 1:1 shows Jesus is eternal and has no beginning. John wrote, "In the beginning was the word."
- *Caution:* Mormons are people who are deceived by false teaching. They are devout in their beliefs and diligent in their efforts to evangelize. It is important to be gentle when confronting false doctrine but also to be armed with truth. Let the Spirit lead you. Make sure you are prepared with Scripture. Help them find the truth.
- The Church of Scientology. A do-it-yourself group founded by a fiction writer L. Ron Hubbard in the 1950s, Scientology calls itself an applied religious philosophy and lists several charismatic Hollywood figures among its membership.
  - ° Beliefs focus on psychological self-help techniques and have very little to say about God, eternal life, sin, or other doctrines.
  - ° Founder, L. Ron Hubbard acknowledged the need to believe in a supreme being, calling that being the "eighth dynamic" or "infinity." Adherents of Scientology who reach the eighth dynamic get to make up their own mind about the eighth dynamic.
  - ° Scientology, like the Mormons and many other cults, masquerades as the true church. They use Christian-sounding terminology. Man becomes his own god. Sin is not a reality; neither is judgment, and truth is found within themselves.
  - ° Looking into self is an empty and fruitless journey that ends in disappointment. The Bible tells us the heart of man is

deceitful above all things (Mark 7:21; Jer. 17:9). Show them the peace that is found in serving the Lord Jesus.

✓ Note: The attack of the enemy in Scientology is against the Godhead, the need for salvation, and the Savior.

- The Watchtower Bible and Tract Society (Jehovah's Witnesses): This group began in the 1870s with Charles Taze Russell. They not only deny the essentials of the Christian faith, but they exercise a high degree of control over the membership.

    ○ The attack of the Enemy is evident in their treatment of the Word of God and their doctrine concerning the deity of Jesus Christ.

    ○ In order to support their false doctrine, the society produced their own version of the Bible, called the "New World Translation." The work deviated substantially from historical translations of the Bible in areas relevant to essential Christian doctrine.

        ▪ Scholars of the day wanted to investigate further, but the Watchtower Society refused to reveal the identity of the translators so their credentials could be examined. After some effort, the members of the translating committee were identified by someone who was part of the headquarters organization at the same time the New World Translation was devised.

        ▪ According to researchers, the New World Bible translation committee had no known translators with recognized degrees in Greek or Hebrew exegesis or translation.

        ▪ None of the members of the committee had any university education, except one, who left school after two years, never completing even an undergraduate degree.

        ▪ There are major differences between the New World Translation and other accepted texts. Of course, all of the differences support the Jehovah's Witnesses' false doctrines.

- ○ What Jehovah's Witnesses believe about Jesus Christ:
  - He is a perfect man created by God.
  - He is a person distinct from God the Father.
  - Before His earthly life, Jesus was a spirit creature, known as Michael the archangel.
  - He became the Messiah at His baptism.
  - Jesus is a mighty one (lesser god), although not almighty, as is Jehovah God.
  - According to John 1:1 in their Bible, the New World Translation, Christ is "a god," but not "the God."
  - They teach that Jesus "was and is and always will be beneath Jehovah" and that "Christ and God are not coequal."
    - ✓ Note: These earnest but deceived people can be seen in all kinds of weather and at all hours, standing on street corners, distributing their material. They are closely monitored by the governing body, which claims to rule with divine authority. Jehovah's Witnesses hope to gain eternal life on earth by their good works. Tell them the truth, and set them free!
- Two more cults you may encounter:
  - ○ Christian Identity Movement (Aryan Nations, Christian Identity Church, Ku Klux Klan). A loose-knit confederation of small groups that are militantly antigovernment and believe in all kinds of government conspiracies. Each group holds differing, deviant Christian-sounding beliefs. All hold to Caucasians being the descendants of the ten "lost" tribes of Israel, God's true people. (It is not likely our Jewish Jesus would pass their racial tests.)
  - ○ The Nation of Islam (Black Muslims). Began in 1930s by W. D. Fard. The group teaches that the black man is good, the white man is the Devil, and that Jesus was merely a prophet. This is also a highly controlling group.

✓ Note: Both Aryan Nation and Black Muslims ignore Scriptures like:
"From one man he made all the nations, that they should inhabit the whole earth; and he marked out their appointed times in history and the boundaries of their lands" (Acts 17:26).

The above list is only a sample.

- A good resource for study of the cults is *Kingdom of the Cults* by Walter Martin. The October 1, 2003, edition was edited by noted Christian apologist Ravi Zacharias and updated with new material by Martin's daughter.
  - *I cannot emphasize this enough!* The existence of Christian-sounding cults is a major reason why the study of true Christian doctrine is essential. We *must* know *what* we believe and *why* we believe it!

What Is the Occult (from a Latin word meaning "hidden")

- Definition of the occult: Any attempt to gain supernatural powers or knowledge apart from the God of the Bible (for example: witchcraft, satanism, psychic activities astrology, séances, tarot cards, Ouija boards).
- Occult activities are blatantly satanic.
  - Some groups blend Christian-sounding names and practices into their rituals to disguise the true source of demonic manifestations. For example, the Caribbean practices of Santeria uses images and names of various saints along with animal sacrifices, chants, and rituals in an attempt to contact God. (We know who they actually contact—the god of this world.)
- The occult is real and dangerous.
  - These are not harmless games played by the curious but a playground for the demonic.
  - Success in the occult brings greater and greater darkness and can ultimately lead to demonic possession.

- The meek and the mild: Some occult practices, like Wicca, masquerade as nature-loving, mild forces, whose goal is to achieve harmony with nature. But in fact, Wicca comes in contact with the same old spirit of darkness behind other more gruesome kinds of occult practices.

  ○ Matt Slick of Christian Apologetics and Research Ministry described how a fascination with Wicca gradually drew him into an anti-Christian attitude. Here is a short section of his testimony:

  Those in Wicca are unwittingly contacting demonic forces and because of that, they gain a form of power. But, that power has a cost. The cost is darkness. I remember very clearly the anti-Christian attitude that gradually grew in me the further into darkness I went. I also remember the fascination with things of darkness such as skulls, pentagrams, the darkness of night, and a general defiant attitude. The more I got involved with that, the more these things increased. There is definitely a spiritual connection with the author of the power behind the occult. Likewise, there is definitely a power that comes from the true and living God, Jesus Christ. He has far more strength, clarity, and truth than anything Wicca can offer. Though the occult is real, God is too; and the only safeguard against the enemy is salvation in Jesus Christ.—Matt Slick, Christian Apologetics and Research Ministry (CARM)

- What the Bible says about occult practices
"When you come into the land which the LORD your God is giving you, you shall not learn to follow the abominations of those nations. There shall not be found among you anyone who makes his son or his daughter pass through the fire, or one who practices witchcraft, or a soothsayer, or one who interprets omens, or a sorcerer, or one who conjures spells, or a medium, or a spiritist, or one who calls up the dead. For all who do these things are an abomination to the LORD" (Deut. 18:9–12a).

- God warns of the ultimate punishment for those who practice such abominations.
  - "Those who practice magic arts ... their place will be in the fiery lake of burning sulfur ... the second death" (Rev. 21:8 NIV).
  - "Those who practice witchcraft (sorcery) will not inherit the kingdom of God" (Gal. 5:20–21 NIV).
  - All these practices are forbidden by God and are acts of rebellion: divination, fortune-telling, mediums, spiritism, necromancy, familiar spirits, wizardry, séances, channeling, clairvoyance, spirit-guides (Deut. 18:9–14; Isa. 44:25; Jer. 27:9; 2 Kings 21:6; 23:24).

Media blitz for the Devil:
- Probably the biggest marketer of occult concepts is the media.
  - Television, video games, and movies show the hero or heroine wielding supernatural powers. Some of these abilities are harmless fantasy (e.g., x-ray vision), while others involve casting spells, using psychic powers, or even contacting spirits.
  - Even popular children's books and movies mix fantasy with the occult, further confusing the problem and positioning children for even greater acts of rebellion against God.
    - ✓ Note: People dabbling in the occult are usually seeking power because they feel powerless. Introduce them to the true power of Jesus Christ.

Tips on ministering to those in the occult (adapted from materials by Campus Crusade for Christ International)
- Understand that the root of occult practice is rebellion against God. God commands that no other god be put before Him.
- When discussing the occult with your friend, be aware of where he/she is spiritually.
  - If your friend has a background in Christianity, using Scripture is appropriate. However, don't start quoting

Leviticus and the stoning of witches to someone who does not reverence the Word of God.

- ° A gentler touch will be more productive. Remember they are probably seeking to fill a big void by gaining the power promised through the occult.
- Recognize the possibility that your friend is seeking a spiritual life and is in need of true guidance.
  - ° Some people play with a Ouija board, looking for a connection with something greater than themselves.
  - ° This motivation is common to those who go to church. We too seek a connection with the one "higher than I" (Ps. 61:2). This may also be your opening to witness.
- Those involved in the occult are sometimes shunned by family and friends.
  - ° Shunning the lost is probably the worst thing a Christian can do.
  - ° Jesus ministered to all kinds of people and embraced those caught up in various destructive behaviors.
- Pray for your friend caught up in the occult.
  - ° This is the best and most productive thing you can do.
  - ° You need to keep yourself immersed in prayer for your own well-being too.
- The occult isn't a game. If your friend is only "playing around," help him/her recognize the seed of rebellion behind the activity.
  - ° Encourage him/her to be thoughtful about his/her spiritual life because spiritual matters aren't a joke.
    - ✓ Note: It is wise to have another Christian accompany you when you are ministering to someone involved in the occult.

The Big New Umbrella—the New Age Movement

- The origin of the movement dates back to at least 1875, with the foundation of the Theosophical Society. The founders were Helena Petrovna Blavatsky and later, in the 1920s, Alice Ann

Bailey, who also founded the Lucifer Publishing Company. (The name should be a clue!)
- The Theosophical Society advocated:
  ◦ Abolishing Christianity, Judaism, and Islam.
  ◦ Promoting the unity of other world religions.
  ◦ They claimed that their teachings were revealed by "spirit" guides (we know them as demons).
  ◦ They emphasized the evolution of a master Aryan society and a one world "New Age" religion and social order (the new world order).
- Bailey's teachings established the symbol of a rainbow as their identification sign.
  ◦ She discussed extensive plans for religious war, forced redistribution of the world's resources, mass planetary initiations, theology for a new world order, worldwide disarmament, and elimination of obstinate religions.
  ◦ She even discussed the sacredness of the new world leader's number, 666 (the number of the Beast)
- Who they are and what they believe.
  ◦ New Agers claim that all mind-science groups are a part of the New Age movement.
  ◦ They also include various occult groups, mystic religions, witchcraft organizations, pagan religions, ecological organizations, and neo-political and secular organizations.
  ◦ New Age is extremely large and is made up of an extensive network of occult leaders devoted to the goals of a forced global government and religion.
  ◦ They openly express their rejection and hostility toward Christianity and other major religions.
  ◦ Their beliefs are similar to many Eastern mystical religions.
  ◦ They seek a universal leader who will fulfill the description of anti-Christ.
- Here are some of the items included in their agenda, according to their manifesto:
  ◦ Establishing a universal government for the new world order.

- ◦ Establishing a universal credit-card system to control finances.
- ◦ Establishing a World food authority to control the food supply.
- ◦ Establishing a World health authority to control medical access.
- ◦ Establishing a World water authority to control water access.
- ◦ Establishing a Universal tax to finance their agenda.
- ◦ Enacting a Universal military draft; all military under one control.
- ◦ Abolishing Christianity, Judaism, and Islam.
- ◦ Anointing a one-world leader.
  - ✓ *Note: Do not fear.* "Even so, when you see these things happening, you know that it is near, right at the door" (Mark 13:29 NIV).

Other Major Religions

- • Unless you live in a neighborhood where many are involved in a particular religion, it is probably not the most profitable use of your time to "specialize." Study the Bible for truth!
  - ◦ There are just too many other religions to discuss all their beliefs. Ask the person to whom you are witnessing about his beliefs and offer to tell him what the Bible says about them.
  - ◦ (Remember, the Holy Spirit is the one who leads into all truth.)
  - ◦ To understand how best to minister to them, ask the two cardinal questions:
    - ▪ Who do you say Jesus is?
    - ▪ What must you do to be saved?
- • Ministering to those of different religions is another reason it is essential for Christians to have a good grasp on God's Word. Become a workman approved unto God (2 Tim. 2:15).

- Although there are too many to cover all other religions, we will cover some basics about Islam, which is a growing presence in many neighborhoods, both in Europe and the United States.

Some basics about Islam and Muslims
- The newest challenge to Christian evangelism in the U.S. is the religion of Islam.
- Most Western Christians know very little about Islam and therefore avoid outreach.
- Basic terminology: the religion is called "Islam"; followers are called, "Muslims."
  - Those who practice Islam are generally very moral people.
- Some Islamic beliefs sound a great deal like Christianity, but don't be deceived into thinking it is the same. For example, Muslims reference and reverence Jesus, but He is not the Son of God. They believe in a different Jesus.
- Salvation in the Islamic religion is based on good works.
  - Christians believe salvation is by grace through faith in the shed blood of Jesus Christ.
  - Forgiveness of sins in Islam is arbitrary and capricious. If Allah wants to forgive sin, he just declares, "It is forgiven."

Christianity recognizes the need for atonement, requiring the shedding of blood for the forgiveness of sin (Heb. 9:22).
- Muslims shed their own blood when they flagellate themselves on certain remembrance days. There is an innate knowledge that blood must be shed, but only the blood of Jesus will cleanse us from sin (1 John 1:7; Matt. 26:28).
- Muslims believe they are saved by performing the five pillars of their faith.
  - Confession of faith: A Muslim must confess, "There is no God but Allah and Mohammed is the prophet of God."
  - Pray: Muslims are required to pray five times a day.
  - Give alms: Muslims are to give about two and one-half percent of their wealth.

- Fast during Ramadan: For one lunar month, from sunrise to sunset, Muslims are not to allow anything to pass down their throats. After sunset, eating is permitted.
- Make a pilgrimage to Mecca: Every Muslim is obligated to travel to the birthplace of Islam (Mecca) once in his or her lifetime.
- Muslims have no guarantee of salvation.
- They believe:
  - their spirit remains in the grave until the day of judgment.
  - all works will be accounted for on the day of judgment.
  - if your bad works outweigh your good works, you will go to hell, but if your good works outweigh your bad works, you'll probably go to heaven.
  - all powerful Allah may do as he pleases; therefore, even the righteous may end up in hell.
  - there is a third possibility for the soul's habitation—a temporary hell. After burning your sins off for a while, you may then be allowed into heaven.
  - Jihadists have the only guarantee of going to heaven.
    - "Jihad" literally means "exerting force for God."
    - A Muslim could be in "jihad" by writing a book about Islam, or by sharing his faith and bringing others to Islam, or by physically fighting for the cause of Islam.
  - Most Muslims are not radicals or even jihadists. The average Muslim is like the average Christian. They know enough to call themselves Muslims but basically just want to live a good and comfortable life.
- Muslims view Christians as immoral because of Western culture.
  - If America is a Christian nation, then everything coming from America must be Christian.
  - We Americans are defined by our immoral movies and TV shows. The country is known as the "great Satan." Because of pornography from the West and the Western media, they equate Christianity with free sex, drugs, alcohol, rape, divorce.

- ◦ The Muslim viewpoint: All the evils of the West confirm their belief that Islam is the true and final religion for all mankind.
- Muslims think Christians believe in three gods: God the Father, God the Son, and God the Mother (Mary).
- They believe Christians and Jews changed the Bible; therefore, existing copies of the Bible can't be trusted.
- They believe the Quran supersedes the Bible.

Special Considerations When Witnessing to Muslims
- An important dynamic in a Muslim's life is a sense of community.
- A Muslim must fit into a larger group to feel safe and secure (for example, an extended family or a network of friends).
- Converts to Christianity report the reasons they previously continued to stay in Islam is only about 10 percent theological but 90 percent cultural.
- Even if they know Christianity is true, they are usually more concerned with leaving the community than truth.
  - ◦ In most Muslim neighborhoods there are no acceptable Christian community alternatives; therefore, a potential convert is exposed.
  - ◦ Muslim Apostasy Laws regarding conversion traditionally required the death penalty, but because there was no clear statement in the Quran, this has been softened in many groups.
  - ◦ However, Muslims who convert to another faith can still be prosecuted.
- Muslim families frequently ostracize converts, treating them as if they actually were dead.

Some tips on witnessing to Muslims from Phil Roberts, director of Interfaith Evangelism. Copyright © 1996 North American Mission Board of the Southern Baptist:
- Be courteous and loving.
- Reflect interest in their beliefs. Allow them time to articulate their views.

- Be acquainted with their basic beliefs.
- Be willing to examine passages of the Qur'an concerning their beliefs.
- Stick to the cardinal doctrines of the Christian faith but also take time to respond to all sincere questions.
- Point out the centrality of the person and work of Jesus Christ for salvation.
- Stress that because of Jesus, His cross, and resurrection, one may have the full assurance of salvation, both now and for eternity (see 1 John 5:13).
- Share the plan of salvation with the Muslim. Point out that salvation is a gift and not to be earned.
- Pray for the fullness of the Holy Spirit. Trust Him to provide wisdom and grace.
- Be willing to become a friend and a personal evangelist to Muslims.

Tips for ministering to people of *all* other religions
- Be respectful of their beliefs, and don't attack them.
- Be aware of differences that affect how they perceive you and Jesus.
  - (For example: Muslims are very sensitive to how they handle the Quran. They believe it is a holy book and will not even carry it below the waistline. Be careful how you handle your Bible. Do not put your Bible on the floor or toss it on a chair.)
- Other religions do not offer their followers much hope. Minister the hope we have in Christ Jesus. We hold the hope of spending eternity in His presence and in the presence of the Father.
- Try to remember, no matter how passionately they maintain their beliefs, they are victims of deception of the Evil One. *You* have the truth—the only truth (John 14:6). Share it in love and humility!

Other Christian Denominations

- Two thousand years of division; ignoring the plea of Paul "Now I exhort you, brethren, by the name of our Lord Jesus Christ, that you all agree, and there be no divisions among you, but you be made complete in the same mind and in the same judgment. For I have been informed concerning you, my brethren, by Chloe's people, that there are quarrels among you. Now I mean this, that each one of you is saying, 'I am of Paul,' and 'I of Apollos,' and 'I of Cephas,' and 'I of Christ'" (1 Cor. 1:10–12).

- Two thousand years of ignoring the plea of Jesus And for their sakes I sanctify myself, that they also might be sanctified through the truth. Neither pray I for these alone, but for them also which shall believe on me through their word; That they all may be one; as thou, Father, art in me, and I in thee, that they also may be one in us: that the world may believe that thou hast sent me. And the glory which thou gavest me I have given them; that they may be one, even as we are one: I in them, and thou in me, that they may be made perfect in one; and that the world may know that thou hast sent me, and hast loved them, as thou hast loved me. (John 17:19–23)

- Some divisions have occurred in Christian churches because of differences in language, ritual, and culture or the methods of teaching of a charismatic personality.

- Like the believers referenced by Paul, they are still of one mind concerning who Jesus is and how one gets saved.
    - Jesus Christ is to be seen as the second person of the Trinity. Paul reminds us that in Him dwells the fullness of the Godhead, bodily (Col. 2:9).
    - Denominations that teach salvation by grace alone, through the mercy of the Father and the work of the crucifixion and resurrection of Jesus Christ, by the action of the Holy Spirit, are focused in the same direction.
    - If we are truly Christians, then we are knit together by a common bond of unity that supersedes denominational

boundaries. There are many people with whom you will disagree over minor matters but stand together on the major doctrines.

- ◦ Remember the two big questions: "Who is Jesus?" and "How do you get saved?"
- John Wesley, founder of the Methodist Church (1703–1791) recorded the following conversation he had, when in a vision he was first transported to hell and later to heaven. (Of course, he referenced denominations that were powerful influences in his day but the principle holds in every age.)

When he saw hell, he asked:

"Are there any Roman Catholics here?" "Yes," came the reply.

"Are there any Presbyterians?" "Yes," was the answer.

"Any Congregationalists?" "Yes."

"Are there any Methodists here?" "Yes," came the reply.

As Wesley thought on this last answer, he was suddenly transported to the gates of heaven. Once again, he called out:

"Are there any Roman Catholics here?" "No," came the reply.

"Are there any Presbyterians?" "No," was the answer.

"Are there any Congregationalists?" "No."

"Are there any Methodists here?" "No," came the reply.

Puzzled, he asked, "Well then, who is here?"

The answer came back, "Christians."

- There are legitimate reasons for division.
  - ◦ Sometimes it is necessary to separate because of serious doctrinal error.
  - ◦ When someone holds to a false teaching or when someone rejects biblical teaching, then it is time to separate.
  - ◦ Example: the Reformation began because of false teaching about salvation and the power of a church to liberate a departed soul from hell.
- Hope for repentance:
  - ◦ Even though a separation has occurred in the past, it is possible for entire groups to repent of false doctrine and return to truth.

- ○ Example: the World Wide Church of God under Herbert W. Armstrong. After Armstrong's death, the new leadership studied the Bible and discovered the false teaching. They repented as a denomination, reestablished fellowship with the rest of Christianity, and changed their name.
- ○ The following is a quote concerning the event from the Apologetics List website.

  On April 3, 2009, the Worldwide Church of God officially changed its name to Grace Communion International. Throughout most of its history, the Worldwide Church of God—founded and led by Herbert W. Armstrong—was, theologically, a cult of Christianity. Among other things, it rejected the doctrine of the Trinity, the bodily resurrection of Jesus, and salvation by grace through faith alone. Sociologically, the movement had many cultic elements as well. However, starting in the mid 1980s under Joseph Tkach Sr., and later his son, Joseph Tkach Jr.—the church's current leader—the Worldwide Church of God has undergone major changes in doctrine to the extent that is has rejected its heretical teachings, and instead has embraced orthodox Christianity.

- The Holy Spirit is the one who activates the heart and leads us into all truth.

  "I have many more things to say to you, but you cannot bear them now. But when He, the Spirit of truth, comes, He will guide you into all the truth; for He will not speak on His own initiative, but whatever He hears, He will speak; and He will disclose to you what is to come. He will glorify Me, for He will take of Mine and will disclose it to you" (John 16:12–14).

- Pray for individuals caught in the grip of false teaching, and pray for entire denominations to be led into biblical truth. You are commanded and empowered to make disciples. You are the light in a very dark world.

  "Let your light so shine before men, that they may see your good works, and glorify your Father which is in heaven" (Matt. 5:16).

For All the Bobs

Someone recently asked what was my heart for *Activate*? That is an easy question to answer. Remember Bob, the man you met in the introduction? Bob loves the Lord with his whole heart and wants to fulfill the Lord's command but does not know how to begin. My heart for *Activate* is to empower all the "Bobs" to become spiritual light in dark places.

Most everyone in this generation recognizes the name of worldwide evangelist Billy Graham, the North Carolina native who took the gospel of Jesus around the globe. I once heard a story about his early life that will help demonstrate my meaning. It seems that before Billy Graham had a relationship with the Lord, he was much like other teenagers, not really into "church stuff." It seems an itinerant evangelist came to his town and set up a tent outside the city limits. The Lord was moving, and people were professing Christ Jesus, but young Billy wanted no part of the meetings. An older man who knew Billy and his family made him an offer he could not refuse. "Bill, come to the meeting, and I will let you drive my new truck." Now, Billy dearly wanted to drive the truck, and so he relented and attended the gospel crusade. The Lord had a better gift for him than driving a truck. God moved upon Billy Graham's heart, and by the time the meeting was over, he had met his Savior. Driving the truck wasn't quite so important anymore.

I can't vouch for the validity of this story, but this I do know. I want to be like the man who offered Billy Graham the use of his truck. Someday, I would like to have a "Bob" tell me that learning skills taught in *Activate* gave him the tools to become a mighty warrior for the Lord Jesus Christ. That's what it is all about—serving the Lord in your generation and helping to equip the next.

ABOUT THE AUTHOR

Thea Spitz was ordained into Christian ministry in 1985 and has served several congregations in outreach evangelism and in teaching the Word. She has the ability to communicate difficult topics in an entertaining and easy-to-grasp manner, inspiring others to follow the command of the Lord to become fishers of men. After spending much of her life in New York City, Thea and her husband now enjoy their country home in a rural community in Virginia.

Printed in the United States
By Bookmasters